CREATING THE NATIONAL PARKS

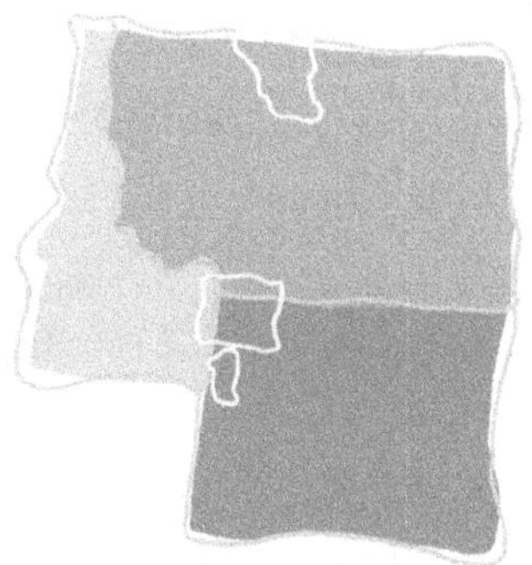

YELLOWSTONE, GLACIER AND GRAND TETON

WILL C. DE MAN

Will C. De Man

Also by Will C. De Man

A Short History of the National Parks: The Southeast

For Atticus and Evander,
who are a "future generation" in the flesh.

Contents

INTRODUCTION

I T ALL GOES BACK to Yellowstone.

This book is about three national parks in the northern Rocky Mountains: Yellowstone, Glacier, and Grand Teton. Though created in three separate eras and under a trio of unique conditions, Yellowstone is like a taproot, the sturdy core from which tendrils branch out and draw these distinct narratives together. These roots supply the philosophical lifeblood that informed parkmaking, wildlife preservation, and forest protection, spiraling out from the geographic center of northwest Wyoming. As a result, the narratives that will play out in the following pages are tied together by central themes, all of which can be traced branching back to the first national park.

The first of these themes is the question of *what a national park should be*. Is it a Garden of Eden or a wilderness? A pleasuring ground or full of hostiles? A place for man or a place for animals? When Yellowstone was created in an act of great foresight in 1872, there was little consensus around any of these questions, and negotiations over the meaning of a national park would play out across the following decades. As new landscapes were considered as heirs to Yellowstone in the national park system—such as Glacier and Grand Teton—new questions emerged. These questions performed like purity tests—ones assessed against the rugged high country of geysers, hot springs and bison.

The second theme is the question of *who is a national park for?* Elite individuals—military officers, businessmen, writers, attorneys, and oil fortune heirs—acted as the driving force to protect Yellowstone, Glacier, and Grand Teton as national parks. In many cases, these elites operated out of their own self-interest and viewed people similar to themselves as the ideal clientele of the national park experience. As will be seen, this resulted in erasure, dispossession, and deep animosity among those who felt they belonged in the landscape—a conviction held just as deeply by the cultural, political, and economic elites who strived for their preservation. As these stories ripple out from the creation of Yellowstone, this too will change. The idealism and altruism that we often associate with national parks—that they have been preserved for *all* Americans—will emerge as efforts transition from personal agendas to the pursuit of an ideal project.

These themes bind the stories of Yellowstone, Glacier, and Grand Teton National Park together, but they also reiterate throughout the history of all our national parks.

The struggle to define the idea of a national park will trigger legislative action, conservationist infighting, and acts of injustice. The negotiation of who the parks are for will produce protests, personal profits, and in some cases, proposals genuinely undertaken for the public good. These are short histories of our national parks—but even in their brevity they demonstrate the influence of these landscapes and the effort to protect them.

YELLOWSTONE NATIONAL PARK

T HERE IS AN AMERICAN mythology of wilderness. This mythology claims that there are strongholds of wild land spread throughout the country, untouched and un-inhabited by man. These primeval pockets range from the Alaskan tundra to the high desert Southwest, fragile in their isolation and in desperate need of protection. If the American people fail to protect these last monuments of land-before-man, they will be consumed by the forces of industry and enterprise. In the 1870s, this mythology became the argument made to protect the wonders of the Yellowstone Plateau as the world's first national park, a designation crafted to create a "pleasuring ground" for the American people that protects its wonders "from injury or spoliation."[1]

In the early history of Yellowstone, this argument was negotiated between the dueling forces of fact and fiction. Over decades, before and after the creation of the national park in 1872, various voices espoused the myth and history that would combine to shape how we understand the origin of Yellowstone National Park. Tall-tales, fact-finding missions, campfire stories, government expeditions—and even outright lies—all played a role in the origin story of the national park. Together, they have created the hazy lens through which we now view Yellowstone—and, to some degree, all national parks.

The interplay between myth and history affects all elements of the Yellowstone origin story, including the deep human past. Unlike what would later be claimed, the Yellowstone Plateau is not a landscape that was devoid of human habitation before the first Euro-American fur trappers snowshoed over the mountain passes. It was a landscape used and respected by ancient people for its resources. As they gathered the things necessary for their survival, these Indigenous ancestors encountered the geysers, hot springs, and strange thermal features that would attract tourists thousands of years later. Their reaction to these geological phenomena was likely the same as the Unites States citizens who campaigned for their protection: awe, wonder, and an understanding that there are greater forces than humankind in the world. In Yellowstone, that through-line of experience—the wonder that places our human existence into the broader context of land and life—is what connects the deep past to the present parkland.

Ancient Days

The first humans to witness the geysers may have been in pursuit of ice-age megafauna (such as wooly mammoths), tracking their prey into the highlands 11,000 years ago.[2] Their visits were only temporary. It would take another 1,500 years of warming temperatures and glacial melt on the Yellowstone Plateau for it to become habitable by humans. About 9,500 years ago, the descendants of the Clovis Culture (a group of ancient human societies that used similar stone tool technology) and other cultures began to make encampments around Yellowstone Lake.

Trends in ancient stone tool technology are often used to identify Paleoindian cultural groups. Changes in the shape of lanceheads, arrow points, knives, and hand axes (also called bifaces) separate distinct groups from one another and represent technological innovations. Clovis points, which are easily identified by their leaf shape and central groove, are considered a technological advancement by the earliest inhabitants of the Americas. The first residents of Yellowstone innovated on Clovis technology, developing what is called the Cody knife. The name comes from a bison kill site discovered just east of Yellowstone near Cody, Wyoming. At this site, points and knives used to butcher the bison have a distinct shape that sets them apart from previous eras and regions. The Cody Culture, as it is called, extended across the Northwest Plains. More than fifty locations throughout Yellowstone

National Park have been linked with the Cody Culture, indicating a widespread and consistent use of the natural resources needed for survival within the highland landscape.[3]

The Cody Culture was probably the first to exploit the invaluable tool-making resource of Yellowstone's Obsidian Cliff, a massive protrusion of volcanic glass in the northwest corner of the park. Through a chemical signature unique to Yellowstone obsidian, archeologists can trace objects found elsewhere directly to Obsidian Cliff. Within the national park and the surrounding territories, numerous sites reveal Cody points produced from Obsidian Cliff material. Over the next several thousand years, the use of obsidian from Yellowstone only increased and "because of its abundance, easy access, and high quality, Obsidian Cliff volcanic glass became one of the most desirable commodities in North American prehistory."[4]

Research performed at the base of Obsidian Cliff makes it clear that ancient peoples didn't just gather obsidian whenever they happened to pass by. Rather, it was something akin to an ancient arrowhead factory. In the 1990s, archeologists walking along Obsidian Cliff observed "thousands of large obsidian cores and bifaces ... strewn across the cliff." At the southernmost end, a 2014 study "observed millions of stone artifacts that attest to the vast amounts of stone tools produced at Obsidian Cliff by Native Americans over the past 11 millennia."[5]

By the Late Archaic period (3,000-1,500 BCE), tools manufactured at Obsidian Cliff dominated Yellowstone, the surrounding regions, and beyond. In the Late Archaic, Great Plains cultures shifted to a heavier reliance on hunting bison, which increased demand for sharp, durable obsidian points. Trade networks spanning across North America ensured that obsidian reached these Plains cultures and beyond. Excavations at the Hopewell Culture Mound City Group in southern Ohio have revealed obsidian artifacts that can be chemically traced back to Obsidian Cliff.[6] This site demonstrates that Yellowstone obsidian was not just a regional commodity, but a continental one. Beyond the Great Plains and Ohio, Yellowstone obsidian has been unearthed throughout the Midwest and as far north as Michigan, Wisconsin, and Ontario.

Beyond just the material value of Yellowstone, its volcanic wonders made their way into Indigenous cultural beliefs as well. Modern tribes such as the Kiowa cast the hot springs and mud pots of Yellowstone as the mythical setting of the creation of their people. The Crow associated bison, a culturally and practically significant animal, with the geysers; they told a story in which the hot breath of the bison formed the steam that erupted from the geysers.

Though the Paleoindian hunter-gatherers long pre-date today's Rocky Mountain tribes, similar cultural practices extended into the modern age. The Sheepeater, or Mountain Shoshone, are one of the many tribes across the Rocky Mountains and Great Plains that utilized the resources of the Yellowstone Plateau. Yellowstone's first superintendent, Philetus Norris, observed that they used "obsidian or volcanic-glass axes" and that Obsidian Cliff was a "weapon and implement quarry."[7] While many Indigenous groups certainly traveled through and hunted within the parkland, the Mountain Shoshone are the only tribe to have called the geothermal highlands home.

They organized their lives around the pursuit of bighorn sheep in the highlands of Idaho, Wyoming, and Montana, thus earning their nickname Sheepeaters. They were semi-nomadic hunters who inhabited Yellowstone in the warmer months and "whose family bands generally followed the migration of the bighorn sheep in much the same way year after year."[8] Because of their cultural practices tied to the remote highlands, cruel stereotypes were crafted to portray the Sheepeaters as subhuman and savage—stereotypes that would be deployed to make a case for the national park itself.

Geyser Lies

Despite clear evidence of long-term human settlement on the Yellowstone Plateau, there was a concerted, decades-long effort by park administrators to erase the Indigenous past. To do so, a myth was concocted—one that was an intentional lie. It claimed that Indigenous communities feared the geysers and hot springs because they didn't understand them, which led them to actively avoid the Yellowstone region. Late into the 20th century, it was commonly believed that "in general, most Indians had a superstitious fear of the geysers and roaring springs, and gave them a wide berth," believing them to be "heap, heap, bad medicine."[9]

In 1928, Horace Albright, superintendent of Yellowstone National Park from 1919 to 1929, wrote: "There were four great tribes of Indians living about the Yellowstone territory. They did not live in Yellowstone, for fear of incurring the wrath of the 'Evil Spirit' who was supposed to reside among the geysers and the hot springs, and also because the country was inaccessible and there was better hunting in the valleys below the park region. The Indian name for the Yellowstone was 'Burning Mountains,' and it is easy to understand their superstitions." Albright's description, which was published in his popular book *Oh, Ranger!*, reflects how deeply ingrained the Geyser Lie (the term I'll use to describe this attempted erasure) became in the half-century after the establishment of the park.[10]

In essence, this deception was concocted as a public relations stunt. Early in the history of the national park, conflict between the federal government and the Native American communities they were trying to subjugate spilled across the boundaries of the newly-minted national park. With the national park idea—indeed, the whole concept of preserving American landscapes for future generations—still in its infancy, early park proponents feared that these conflicts would hurt the public view of Yellowstone National Park, deter visitation, and ultimately doom the park project.

The first of a sequence of tragic events involved the Ne-Mee-Poo, or Nez Perce, whose ancestral homelands were west of the park boundary. The Nez Perce were forced out of their homelands by unsuccessful and coercive treaties. Tensions between factions within the Nez Perce and the federal government sparked violence, which prompted a mass exodus led by Chief Joseph. He planned to traverse the Rocky Mountains with his people, aiming to join Sitting Bull and an enclave of Lakota refugees across the Canadian border. The flight of these refugees, pursued by 2,000 U.S. soldiers, brought fear and violence into Yellowstone National Park just five years after it was created.

On August 24, 1877, the flight of the Nez Perce intersected with a group of tourists from Radersburg, Montana. This group, known as the Radersburg Party, included seven men and two women. After a tense interchange, violence erupted between the Nez Perce and the tourists: one man was shot in the leg, another in the face. Both men survived, but the party was taken captive by the Nez Perce. Several members managed to escape and those who remained were released after several harrowing days.

Shortly after, the Helena Party—a separate sight-seeing expedition of ten men—watched the Nez Perce pass through the Lamar Valley. The exodus of Indigenous refugees was so large that the Helena Party first mistook them for a herd of elk. The Nez Perce learned the location of the Helena Party, and a group of scouts soon approached to steal the party's provisions. Again, there was gunfire: one man was killed, another shot in the hip. A final violent encounter occurred on August 31 when the remnants of the Helena Party and others fended off a band of Nez Perce warriors at the Mammoth Hot Springs Hotel.[11]

Mammoth Hot Springs, 1871, William Henry Jackson. Courtesy National Park Service History Collection.

In the early days of Yellowstone National Park, these events did not appear to be isolated. The following year, in 1878, starvation conditions on the Fort Hall reservation led to conflict between the U.S. Army and the Bannock Tribe. This conflict bled across the boundaries of the park and a contingency of men under the authority of Yellowstone Superintendent Philetus Norris were involved. In 1879, it appeared imminent that a third war would cross the park boundary as the federal government battled the Mountain Shoshone in Idaho. Though this conflict never spread to Yellowstone, park officials and promoters feared that the "nation's playground had become a yearly battleground."[12]

These violent encounters between Indigenous people, tourists, and soldiers were terrible publicity for the newborn national park. In the late 1800s, many Americans were spending their summer vacations in Europe, taking in the Alps and the Rhine. If the American West—which was becoming more open to settlers and sightseers alike—was going to compete, it had to be made safe for tourists. From the perspective of park promoters, it was necessary to scrub Yellowstone clean of Native Americans, past and present. It is from this "necessity" that the Geyser Lie was born. In his 1877 report to the Secretary of the Interior, Yellowstone Superintendent Norris wrote:[13]

"The lamentable Indian raid, burning of houses, bridges, and massacre of innocent tourists within the park...is as anomalous as unexpected; the first, and probably the last of the kind, as it is wholly aside from all Indian routes, and only chosen in the desperation of retreat by the Nez Perces, who have acquired sufficient civilization and Christianity to at least overpower their pagan superstitious fear of earthly fire-hole basins and brimstone pits."

In just a few sentences, Norris dismisses the violence as a fluke and deploys stereotypes of Indigenous people as uncivilized savages to support his claims. Later in his report, he makes the case again. This time he includes imagery of the Yellowstone wilderness as a Garden of Eden, full of majestic and peaceful creatures that form a powerful contrast to the "Sheep-eater":

"Owing to the isolation of the park, deep amid snowy mountains, and the superstitious awe of the roaring cataracts, sulphur pools, and spouting geysers, over the surrounding pagan Indians, they seldom visit it, and only a few harmless Sheep-eater hermits, armed with bows and arrows, ever resided there, and even they now vanished. Hence in no other portion of the West or of the world was there such an abundance of elk, moose, deer, mountain sheep, and other beautiful and valuable animals, fish and fowl."

Norris does not claim that mankind *never* resided in Yellowstone—just that the few who did were much less than civilized and of little importance. Throughout his tenure as the Superintendent of Yellowstone National Park, Norris wrote of the Sheepeaters in utterly dehumanizing ways. He describes the Mountain Shoshone as physically subhuman, calling them a "pygmy" tribe. Their culture is also disparaged, being referred to as reclusive "hermits" who continue to use primitive technology, "armed with bows and arrows."[14]

The creation of these stereotypes was ultimately done in service of the Geyser Lie. The humanity of the Mountain Shoshone—and the evidence of long-term habitation—undermined the central element of this public relations mythology. It couldn't be claimed that the Native Americans were afraid of the geysers if they'd been living among them all along. Thus, they had to be painted as uncivilized and feeble brutes, too overcome by the primal instincts that prompted them to fear the geothermal features. It was intended to be a powerful contrast against the scientists and artists whose documentation of the landscape would lead to its protection. It's a story that fit with the popular narrative that was told as awareness of Yellowstone grew: that it was a strange, otherworldly place shrouded in steam and sulfur, a place that could surely only exist in the imagination of those who might not be entirely civilized themselves.

Mountain Man Mythologies

The Geyser Lie was just one element of the many myths that developed around the creation of Yellowstone. The difficulty of splitting fact from fairytale in this mysterious part of the Northern Rockies traces back to the start of the 19th century, long before the idea of a national park was conceived. With the acquisition of the Louisiana Territory from France, President Thomas Jefferson was eager to launch a fact-finding mission into the western part of the continent. Led jointly by Captain Meriwether Lewis and Lieutenant William Clark, the Corps of Discovery set out from St. Louis on May 14, 1804, and embarked up the Missouri River. Their goal was to gather scientific information about this previously un-surveyed land and hopefully determine a maritime trade route between the Mississippi River and the Pacific Ocean.

To be a member of Lewis and Clark's expedition, individuals had to be "good hunters, stout, healthy, unmarried men, accustomed to the woods and capable of bearing bodily fatigue in a pretty considerable degree."[15] Throughout Lewis and Clark's treacherous fact-finding mission, John Colter, a private in the Corp of Discovery, displayed these qualities to the utmost. Through the transcontinental journey, he proved to be hardy, skilled, and of good sense. These attributes would play out in casting Colter as the main character of the first entry in the Yellowstone storybook—an entry that would be shrouded in decades of uncertainty as to whether it belongs to the genre of fantasy or fact.

Returning from the Pacific with the Corps of Discovery in 1806, Colter was presented with a lucrative business opportunity. Two frontiersmen, Forrest Hancock and

Joseph Dickson, were paddling back up the Missouri River to begin a beaver trapping operation. After receiving permission from his captains, Colter opted to join them. He did business with them for a season, later joining the outfit of Manuel Lisa, a Spaniard who established a trading post at the junction of the Bighorn and Yellowstone rivers. Colter was commissioned to be his publicist, trekking into the Rocky Mountain interior to inform the mountain tribes that the trading post was open for business. It was this event that would turn Colter into Yellowstone's first mythical hero.

John Colter began his marketing campaign in the winter of 1807, initially traveling down the Yellowstone River. Eventually, he passed through what would become both Yellowstone and Grand Teton national parks—making him the first Euro-American to witness both world-famous landscapes. The hard evidence of Colter's journey and accomplishment is scant, but it has stood up under two-hundred years of scrutiny. Colter left behind no diaries or maps. With no direct account from Colter, the best evidence for the accuracy of his journey comes from a map created by William Clark some years later. The two men reunited in St. Louis, where Colter either dictated or drew his route for Clark. Published in 1814, the map displayed the Yellowstone and Grand Teton region, with a dotted line approximating Colter's journey.

If the path marked by William Clark is accurate, Colter deserves a seat in the pantheon of great western explorers; if it isn't, then perhaps Colter's place is seated among the greatest fibbers in history. There will always be an air of uncertainty around Colter's true route because he did not give "a detailed account of his trip to any of the several competent writers he encountered, [or make] certain that his family or friends were able to preserve either his own written version or a crude sketch of his route. In fact, it is not known whether Colter drew a map for William Clark, or just told him of the route."[16] Even if Clark's map is to be trusted, many of its physical features are distorted or out of scale, making it difficult to determine exactly the route Colter took.

Despite the uncertain details of his route, the legend of John Colter's harrowing journey through Yellowstone was told as if it was true. Colter himself was the source of the tale, spreading it among friends and family. As the story spread beyond his immediate circles, it grew into the fireside fable of "Colter's Hell," an infernal landscape where tar bubbled out of the ground, flames leapt from cracks in the rock, and the air smelled of sulfur. One can't help but imagine the brave John Colter, a handkerchief held over his mouth as he choked through the fumes and dodged boiling puddles. As the details of his story transformed more of what he saw into a wilderness hellscape, Colter's fame could have erupted like a geyser in some circles; in others, his reputation may have plummeted. He was a legend—but it was hard to tell whether he was the hero of an epic expedition or simply an attention-seeking storyteller. Today, his journey is an icon as the first of a series of explorations that would ultimately result in the creation of the first national park.

Expeditions to Fairyland

Though several other Euro-American trappers would traverse the Yellowstone Plateau in the six decades after his journey, the reputation of John Colter's story as a mountain man mythology persisted. Many didn't take Colter's story seriously, thinking it far too fantastic to be true. A desire not to be associated with these allegations played a role in stunting serious exploration of the northwest corner of the Wyoming territory. The difficult highland terrain, mixed with convictions among some that Colter's tale was fiction, made an investigation of his claims more trouble than they were worth for decades.

Eventually, curiosity in the frontier towns of the west prompted a legitimate investigation of the territory around "Colter's Hell"—one that would be very carefully documented. The first expedition with the specific intent of exploration launched in the fall of 1869. A small party of only three men—David Folsom, Charles Cook, and William Peterson—departed from Diamond City, Montana, on September 6. The Folsom party spent a month exploring the Yellowstone region, recording their observations of Yellowstone Lake, the Lower Geyser Basin, and the Grand Canyon of the Yellowstone. Upon their return, Folsom and Cook poured over their diaries, collaborating to produce a map and a narrative account of their journey. Folsom reluctantly allowed their account to be published in the *Western Monthly Magazine*. Because of Yellowstone's notoriety as a fur-trapper's fable, he feared that publicizing the story of their expedition could harm his reputation.

Though Folsom and Cook's account was met with skepticism, others were intrigued and inspired by it. A second mission was quickly organized to probe the geothermal wonderland. The sulfurous miasma of mystery over the region was slowly beginning to lift for Euro-Americans. Following a successful military and political career, Henry Washburn was appointed surveyor general of the Montana Territory. He was determined to lead an expedition into Yellowstone to produce more accurate maps of the region. To entice more men to sign on to his expedition, a military detachment under Lieutenant Gustavus Doane of the 2nd U.S. Cavalry at Fort Ellis was organized to join Washburn. There was a broad fear of raids by tribes such as the Blackfeet, and the promise of a protective escort helped encourage more men to join the Washburn expedition.

In addition to Washburn and Doane, a third significant member signed onto this second expedition into Yellowstone. Nathaniel Pitt Langford joined the party as an associate of the floundering Northern Pacific Railroad. As the west opened up, railroad companies were often award-ed land leases by the federal government. In exchange for these leases, it was expected that railways would be built that promoted settlement, improved the economy, and connected the ever-expanding nation. The Northern Pacific Railway company was at risk of losing its lease and needed to construct a profitable railway line in the northwest. Jay Cooke, a financier of the railroad, heard ru-mor of Yellowstone's wonders and imagined an incredible business opportunity. If the tall tales of the mountain men were true, Yellowstone had serious potential as a tourist destination to rival Niagara Falls and Mammoth Cave. If the Northern Pacific could be the first to build a rail line to Yellowstone, it could essentially monopolize access to its wonders.

The Washburn Party used the map produced by Fol-som and Cook and left Bozeman, Montana, on August 11, 1870 A month into their expedition, tragedy struck. On September 9, Truman Everts became separated from the group. While his companions put up a valiant search for him, Everts was considered lost in the vast, mostly unknown wilderness of the Yellowstone Plateau. Accord-ing to his later account in *Scribner's Monthly*, Everts ex-perienced "a crushing sense of destitution. No food, no fire; no means to procure either; alone in an unexplored wilderness, one hundred and fifty miles from the nearest human abode, surrounded by wild beasts, and famishing with hunger. It was no time for despondency. A moment afterwards I felt how calamity can elevate the mind, in the formation of the resolution 'not to perish in that wilderness.'"[17]

Everts's resolve remained strong even as he lost his horse, along with all his tools and weapons. He set off in the wrong direction, failing to find his companions. He began an aimless odyssey, surviving off scraps of birds and elk thistle. "I tasted it," he wrote. "It was palatable and nutritious. My appetite craved it."[18] His wanderings in the wilderness were filled with misadventure; he was treed by a mountain lion, seriously scalded in a hot spring, sparked a minor forest fire, and hallucinated visions of an old cleric who guided him through the wilderness. When Everts was finally rescued, he had been lost in the Upper Yellowstone region for thirty-seven days.

Departing from Folsom's route, the Washburn Party trekked into the Upper Geyser Basin, which was previously unknown to Euro-Americans. Upon entering, they were greeted by the most iconic feature in the entire national park system. Nathaniel Langford wrote, "we saw in action on entering the basin, ejected from a crevice of irregular form, and about four feet long by three wide, a column of water of corresponding magnitude to the height of one hundred feet."[19] As they observed the geyser, Henry Washburn took note of the regular intervals at which the geyser "played." He dubbed it Old Faithful. The Washburn expedition also named the Beehive, Castle, Fan, Giant, Giantess, and Grotto geysers, titling them to "best illustrate their peculiarities."[20]

Old Faithful, 1883, William Henry Jackson. Courtesy of the NPS History Collection.

On September 19, lacking supplies and their lost companion, the party made the decision to begin the journey out of Yellowstone (Truman Everts wouldn't be rescued for another month). When they returned to Helena, Montana, members of the party swiftly began to prepare accounts of their journey to share with the public. With the Folsom-Peterson account now corroborated, hesitation about being labeled a liar for claiming to witness boiling mud pots seems to have dispersed. Reports of the expedition were published across the country, including in the *Weekly Rocky Mountain Gazette* and *New York Times*.[21] Gustavus Doane, as a member of the U.S. Army and escort for the trip, prepared an official government report. For the sake of his sponsors, Nathaniel Pitt Langford prepared a 13,000-word lecture that advocated for the creation of a Northern Pacific Railroad line to deliver tourists to Yellowstone. Presenting his remarks in both Montana and the East, he claimed that the Northern Pacific could "render this remarkable region of natural wonders, accessible [sic]" in just a three-day journey from the major eastern cities.[22]

In a sense, the unverifiable story of John Colter was like an acorn dropping into a still pond. It was the first event that ultimately led toward a thorough exploration of one of the last unknown landscapes in the United States. Told around the fireplace on winter nights, the stories about "Colter's Hell" were a fairytale—until more credible men confirmed it as nonfiction. The mystery of the region attracted the Folsom Party, whose account in turn prompted the Washburn Expedition. Each exploration only grew in intensity and detail—a trend that continued with the final mission into the volcanic landscape. It was this final expedition that would finally inspire the creation of a national park.

Scientists and Painters

On January 19, 1871, the head of the U.S. Geological Survey and Geographical Survey of the Territories listened to Nathaniel Langford's address in Washington, D.C. His name was Ferdinand V. Hayden and he would lead the third and final expedition before Yellowstone became a national park. After Washburn and Langford publicized their accounts, Hayden was given a directive from the Secretary of the Interior, Columbus Delano, to explore the Yellowstone region. This was a major development in the exploration of a geography that had been dismissed as tall tales just a few years prior. All previous explorations had been motivated by the curiosity of frontiersmen, those living just beyond Yellowstone's hot gates. Hayden's mission was the first to take place on a national scale, sponsored by the federal government.

Significantly, it would also be the first mission into Yellowstone with the express goal of gathering scientific data. This was a luxury afforded by the previous expedition. Now that there was less of a burden to confirm the mythical geysers, they could be studied. The Hayden expedition would incorporate a diverse range of scientists including a geologist, entomologist, botanist, zoologist, and meteorologist. Most unique of all, the Hayden expedition involved photographers and painters tasked with creating visual proof of Yellowstone's oddities. To dispel the disbelief of the general public, the written word needed to be accompanied by visual proof—proof of both the reality of the region and the beauty of its sights.

The Hayden Survey, 1871, William Henry Jackson. Courtesy of the NPS History Collection.

Like Nathaniel Langford's role in the Washburn expedition, the interests of the Northern Pacific were served by the presence Thomas Moran, of one of the artists. The railroad paid to have the painter join Hayden's crew to create sketches of the landscape that would be source material for full-size paintings. The Northern Pacific Railroad intended to use these paintings to excite the public about Yellowstone—a public they intended to serve via their own railway. In a letter to Hayden, Jay Cooke made it clear that Thomas Moran's inclusion was ultimately intended to benefit the corporation: "I think that Mr. Moran will be a very desirable addition to your expedition, and it will be a great accommodation to our house [Jay Cooke & Co.] & the [rail]road, if you will assist him in his efforts."[23]

As the Hayden survey began its official exploration in July 1871, the secrets of Yellowstone continued to reveal themselves. After traveling up the Gardner River, the survey found itself at the terraces of Mammoth Hot Springs, a spectacular formation that neither the Folsom nor Washburn parties had encountered. From there they followed a similar path as the Washburn expedition, past Yellowstone Lake. All along the way, the disciplines of science and art worked in tandem to record the wonders of Yellowstone. While Hayden's scientists recorded data, Moran and the photographer William Henry Jackson collected visual specimens in the form of sketches and copper plates. In just three years, the fog of secrecy shrouding the Yellowstone Plateau had been thoroughly burned away by exploration and survey.

Campfire Fables

While the idea to establish a national park was not new, it did not gain traction until after the Hayden survey was completed. Continuing to advocate in their own interest behind the scenes, the Northern Pacific Railroad sent a letter to Hayden upon his return to the east. A.B. Nettleton, assistant to Jay Cooke, wrote that there was a "suggestion which strikes me as being an excellent one... Let Congress pass a bill reserving the Great Geyser Basin as a public park forever—just as it has reserved that far inferior wonder the Yosemite valley and big trees."[24] Hayden responded positively to the suggestion. He and members of all three expeditions into Yellowstone would become enthusiastic supporters and advocates for a public park.

In 1871 there was a great sense of urgency around the withdrawal of Yellowstone from the public domain. Overshadowing the budding conservation movement was the ugly specter of Niagara Falls. The natural scenery of the falls had been all but sacrificed to private tourism and industry. Its rim was crowded with hotels, advertisements, and scams, all looking to profit off the churning roar of the falls dumping over the Niagara escarpment. It was a prescient lesson in what not to do with powerful scenery: if given the opportunity, private interests would extract every penny from the public who wished to see it.

Similarly, a lesson had been learned from the creation of the Yosemite Reserve. Established as a national park precursor in California in 1864, the government had struggled to remove settlers from the valley floor. The case eventually moved to the Supreme Court. Their final ruling removed settlers from the floor of Yosemite Valley on the grounds that they had not fully complied with homesteading law before the Reserve was established. As Folsom, Washburn, and Hayden's reports made the public more aware of Yellowstone, the risk of private land claims became more likely. If this was allowed to occur, Yellowstone would be condemned to a future of overpriced tickets and gaudy advertisements—transformed into Colter's *tourist* hellscape.

According to the diary of Nathaniel Pitt Langford, that was nearly the fate of Yellowstone's wonders. He recounts a fireside conversation among members of the Washburn expedition held on the final day of their journey. A topic of discussion was the future of the landscape: "the proposition was made by some members that we utilize the result of our exploration by taking up quarter sections of land at the most prominent points of interest."[25] This suggestion would mean filing claims on the geyser fields and hot springs, fencing off the shores of Yellowstone Lake and establishing homesteads on the edge of the Grand Canyon of Yellowstone. Like Niagara Falls, members of the Washburn expedition suggested developing the marvels of the Yellowstone Plateau for tourism, making themselves rich by monopolizing its majesty.

This could have been the disastrous fate of Yellowstone (and perhaps the death of the budding national park movement), if not for the apparent heroism of one member of the group. According to Langford, Cornelius Hedges, a Montanan lawyer, chastised the party and said "that there ought to be no private ownership of any portion of that region, but that the whole of it ought to be set apart as a National Park."[26] Supposedly Hedges' righteous indignation was enough to quickly persuade the party that the preservation of Yellowstone was the only acceptable outcome of their journey. Langford wrote that Hedges was met with "an instantaneous and favorable response from all—except one—of the members of our party, and each hour since the matter was first broached, our enthusiasm has increased."[27]

A re-enactment of the campfire story, 1957, John Tyers. Courtesy of the NPS History Collection.

Like the fireside story of Colter's Hell, the factual nature of the "Campfire Story" is dubious. Like the Geyser Lie, it was considered to be historically authentic for decades, espoused by park officials and commemorated by an annual re-enactment at the confluence of the Firehole and Gibbon rivers. Though ultimately an origin myth, the Campfire Story has a practical function: it's useful in its ability to communicate the feelings and philosophy that motivated the creation of the national park.

Reserving Yellowstone

While the Campfire Story is only an entertaining fable, the true establishment of the world's first national park is just as fascinating in the way it deals with the same individuals and issues. Cornelius Hedges, Nathaniel Pitt Langford, and Ferdinand V. Hayden were instrumental in the campaign to protect Yellowstone, the latter two lobbying Congress directly in the East while Hedges campaigned in the Montana Territory. Both Langford's article in *Scribner's Monthly* and Hayden's official report on Yellowstone were made available to members of Congress. Hayden organized specimens collected during his survey to be displayed alongside the sketches of Thomas Moran and photographs of William Henry Jackson in the rotunda of the Capitol. This made it possible for members of Congress to have an almost first-hand experience of Yellowstone without making the cross-country journey themselves.

All this work garnered enthusiasm from preservation-minded members of Congress, who began drafting legislation in December 1871. At first, it seemed that the withdrawal of Yellowstone would be built on the model of the 1864 Yosemite Reserve. It was proposed that a Yellowstone Reserve be created for the Territory of Montana, just as the Yosemite Reserve had been created for California. This proved politically toxic because the majority of land to be preserved lay inside the Wyoming Territory, with thin edges bleeding over into Idaho and Montana. Thus, it was resolved that Yellowstone should be called a national park and should remain under the authority of the federal government, rather than any individual territory. With this seemingly mundane semantic and bureaucratic decision, the national park system that would grow over the coming century was conceived.

Though the Campfire Story has been debunked, the threat of private settlement was a major motivation in the quick creation of Yellowstone National Park. As part of the argument to prevent settlers from staking claims in Yellowstone, it had to be made clear that Yellowstone was ill-suited for any sort of agricultural production. Massachusetts Rep. Henry Dawes made the case, stating "[Yellowstone] is a region of country seven thousand feet above the level of the sea, where there is frost every month of the year, and where nobody can dwell upon it for the purpose of agriculture." From Henry Dawes's perspective, the only reason a settler could want to stake a homestead in Yellowstone was to profit off its wonders—just as the Washburn Expedition had supposedly schemed in the account of Nathaniel Langford.[28]

On January 30, 1872, the bill to create Yellowstone National Park was passed by the U.S. Senate. Two months later, it passed in the House of Representatives. On March 1, 1872, less than a year after the return of the Hayden expedition, President Ulysses S. Grant signed the legislation establishing Yellowstone National Park. From the Folsom Party in 1869 to President Grant's signing in 1872, the protection of Yellowstone was swift and decisive. If Langford's Campfire Story is to be believed, those who witnessed its wonders overwhelmingly agreed that it must be protected for all Americans to enjoy. The law creating Yellowstone National Park set the mandate that has echoed through the history of our national parks ever since: that it would be "a public park or pleasuring-ground for the benefit and enjoyment of the people" and it is the duty of the federal government to "provide for the preservation, from injury or spoliation, of all timber, mineral deposits, natural curiosities, or wonders with said park, and their retention in their natural condition" and to "provide against the wanton destruction of the fish and game found within said park."[29]

Fulfilling this legal obligation was a tall order in a high-elevation wilderness covering more than two million acres. Over the next several decades, as the conservation movement burgeoned, additional laws would be passed to protect the wildlife and natural features of America's first national park. Shortly after its establishment, it was determined that Yellowstone needed a superintendent to manage its protection and visitation. The story of Truman Everts's thirty-seven days of misfortune in Yellowstone had appeared, with stunning illustrations, in the November 1871 issue of *Scribner's Monthly*. A well-known and popular figure associated with Yellowstone, Everts's experience with Yellowstone's landscape certainly had no rivals. With such an intimate knowledge of the terrain, he would have been an excellent first superintendent and was offered the job. He declined.

GLACIER NATIONAL PARK

G LACIER NATIONAL PARK, A crown jewel in the National Park System, is defined by three divides. The first is the Continental Divide, the geographic split which forms the spectacular scenery of walled-in lakes, triangular peaks, and expansive glaciers. It cuts straight through the heart of Glacier, separating the waters of the continent by draining to the Pacific in the west and the Atlantic in the east. The second divide that characterizes the park is the political border between Canada and the United States. In the wilderness of the Northern Rockies, this border is entirely arbitrary; it holds no authority over the movement of wildlife, the run of rivers, or the spread of wildfire. On the other side of the U.S.-Canada border, directly adjacent to Glacier, is Canada's Waterton Lakes National Park. In 1932 the two parks were forever entwined as an International Peace Park, uniting geopolitical allies and wilderness ecosystems.

The third divide is that of human tragedy. It is the division of a people from their homeland. To the east of the

Continental Divide, the Great Plains stretch for hundreds of miles. Together with the mountains of the Northern Rockies, they formed the homeland of what was once the most formidable Indigenous nation in the Upper West. They were three distinct tribes—the Blackfeet, Piegan, and Kainah—known together as the Blackfeet Nation. As the Indigenous people most often associated with Glacier, the Blackfeet were used to market the national park as a romantic reminder of the Wild West. Tribesmen in full regalia were employed to greet tourists descending the steps of the Great Northern Railway platform, their teepees pitched on the lawns of the luxurious hotels built by Louis Hill. This paternalistic practice was not the worst crime committed against the Blackfeet in the name of Glacier National Park. In order for the park to be created, the Blackfeet first had to be betrayed by an ally and divided from their ancestral homeland.

A Blackfeet encampment at Logan Pass, 1933, George A. Grant. Courtesy Montana Historical Society.

The Most Formidable Nation in the West

The Blackfeet were not the only Indigenous communities to make use of the significant natural resources found in the Northern Rockies. The territory to the west of the Continental Divide was home to the Salish, Kootenai and Pend d'Oreilles. Like the Blackfeet, they relied on the mountains that would become Glacier National Park. Their ways of living depended on migrating into the Rocky Mountain highlands in the warm months to hunt game, gather plants, and cut timber. When these resources became scarce, it prompted skirmishes with the Blackfeet, who became well known as formidable warriors and cunning strategists. The Blackfeet often targeted the horses of enemy tribes, stealing them and thus limiting the ability of rival Indigenous parties to travel long distances with heavy loads. From the time that Lewis and Clark's Corp of Discovery made contact with them, relations between the Blackfeet Nation and the U.S. government were tense. Wagon trains making their way through the Great Plains skirted well beyond Blackfeet territory, hoping to avoid Blackfeet warriors who were quick to defend their homeland.

In 1855, Washington Territory Governor Isaac Ingalls Stevens invited the Salish, Kootenai, and Pend d'Oreilles to a treaty negotiation near present-day Missoula, Montana. While they'd hoped that a treaty with the United States would protect them from the Blackfeet, the three tribes soon realized Stevens's true goal: to dispossess them of their land. Though they attempted to dispute the terms of their treaty, the power imbalance between the Indigenous communities and the United States government ultimately resulted in a cession of nearly all their land and authority. Caught between the Blackfeet and the United States government, the three tribes had no choice but to sign the Treaty of Hellgate. It established a reservation on the Flathead River for what would become the Confederated Salish and Kootenai Tribes.

That same year, Governor Stevens turned his attention across the Continental Divide toward the formidable Blackfeet. Meeting at the Judith River, the treaty negotiation was a showdown between two great powers of the Upper West. Stevens had a reputation for dealing brutally with tribes that resisted him; the Blackfeet were the most formidable tribe west of the Black Hills. The terms of the treaty reflected the considerable power of both sides. A massive Blackfeet reservation was agreed upon, stretching over 17 million acres and bounded by the Continental Divide, the Canadian border, and the Missouri River. Part of the land would be reserved as a common hunting ground for all nearby tribes. Yearly payments would be provided to the Blackfeet to help them become "civilized." In return for the money and land promised in the treaty, white settlers were guaranteed safe passage through the reservation and the U.S. government would be allowed to construct transportation and communication infrastructure within it.

While the Blackfeet retained a massive territory and received cash payments, the treaty was seeded with terms intended to slowly erode their cultural identity and claims to the land. Rather than just passing safely through, white settlers soon began squatting on land within the Blackfeet reservation. Roads and railroads brought prospectors and settlers, along with the infrastructure necessary to make their lives more comfortable. White settlers pressured the federal government to open up more land by shrinking the Blackfeet reservation. This was enacted by executive order in 1871, a loss for which the Blackfeet were not compensated.[1]

Perhaps most insidious of the treaty terms were the requirements for how the Blackfeet spent the cash payments made to them by the federal government: $20,000 annually to purchase goods and provisions on the market, $15,000 to fund a transition towards agriculture and mechanization.[2] These requirements were an intentional strategy to erode traditional Indigenous lifeways on the Blackfeet reservation. Relying on purchased goods and practicing mechanized agriculture were a far cry from the semi-nomadic, bison-hunting lifeway of the Blackfeet culture. It was an intentional act of cultural destruction. By disconnecting the Blackfeet from the natural resources of the mountains, plains, and bison, the U.S. Government intended to dilute their cultural identity.

The authority of the once indomitable Blackfeet declined sharply over the next four decades. The loss of a strong cultural identity, collapse of bison populations, ravages of smallpox, and reliance on shipments of provisions resulted in starvation and poverty: "Whereas once the tribe had been mobile and mighty, living in cooperative bands, families now hunkered in painful poverty along the southern boundary of the reservation to be closer to the meager government annuities that they were now dependent upon for survival."[3] As outsiders witnessed the once-feared Blackfeet nation brought to its knees by the official policy of the federal government, some saw it as an opportunity to exploit the hidden riches of the mountains within the western part of the reservation. The division of the Blackfeet from their land was fully underway.

In 1895, the diminished Blackfeet were approached with an opportunity to once again exchange their land for cash. A man of many "talents," James Willard Schultz was married to a Blackfeet woman and lived among them. He guided hunters in the mountains, traded whiskey, and had written a collection of Blackfeet stories for the outdoor magazine *Forest and Stream*. However, he was also interested in prospecting on the Blackfeet's reserved portion of the Rocky Mountains. He wrote to a political contact in Washington, D.C., relaying rumors of gold located in the mountains.[4] The rumors spread among both the Blackfeet

Nation and Congress. Each became convinced that there was a wealth of gold, silver, copper and oil in the mountains, despite the skepticism of Interior Secretary Hoke Smith. Negotiations for opening up the "mineral strip" of the Blackfeet reservation began in September 1895. The Department of the Interior commissioned three men to forge an agreement with the Blackfeet. Chief among them was a man well known in the tribe, George Bird Grinnell.

The Many-Faced Preservationist

George Bird Grinnell is an elder god in the pantheon of American conservationists, seated beside the likes of John Muir, Theodore Roosevelt, and Horace Albright. Throughout his adult life, Grinnell would leave the comforts of his upper-crust elite lifestyle and foray into the rugged American West. These summer adventures first began after he graduated from Yale in 1870 when he spent six months gathering fossils for the Peabody Museum. In 1874, he joined the military expedition of George Armstrong Custer into the Black Hills as a naturalist. The following year, he applied his naturalist skills to a U.S. Army survey of Yellowstone. In 1885, he was guided by James Willard Schultz through the Northern Rockies and experienced the piled-up mountains and walled-in lakes of Glacier for the first time.[5] Grinnell was enraptured by the region, visiting year after year and attaching his own name, as well as the names of his companions, to the peaks, lakes, and glaciers that composed the stunning scenery.

George Bird Grinnell atop Grinnell Glacier c. 1925. Tomar Hileman, courtesy of the Montana Historical Society.

Like many modern environmental advocates, Grinnell's experiences in the wilderness prompted a deep passion for its protection. While the establishment of Glacier National Park may be his greatest credit, Grinnell's environmental legacy stretches far beyond it. Raised on the former estate of ornithologist John James Audubon, it could be said that protecting the natural world was Grinnell's birthright. He denounced the use of bird plumage in high fashion by forming the first Audubon Society.

Together with future president Theodore Roosevelt, he formed the Boone and Crockett Club to defend large game such as elk, bison, and antelope. His primary occupation was as the editor of the weekly magazine *Forest and Stream*, championing every preservationist cause that caught his eye. The publication functioned as his bully pulpit, from which he was able to score significant victories for the early American conservation movement, including multiple victories in Yellowstone National Park.

Like the treaty rights of the Blackfeet, Yellowstone was only protected in writing and faced many practical threats. In the early 1890s, Grinnell lobbied both politicians and the public through *Forest and Stream*, strongly advocating for preserving the natural integrity of the park. In 1891, a massive victory was achieved through the passage of the Forest Reserve Act, a law that Grinnell and "nearly every advocate for wilderness and wildlife had been pushing for many years."[6] The Forest Reserve Act allowed the president to unilaterally set aside expanses of timberland as forest reserves. This law effectively placed a conservation shield on large tracts of wild lands, allowing the federal government to control exactly what type of industry occurred in them.

Though Yellowstone was a massive park at more than two million acres, Grinnell and others felt it wasn't fully protected from hunters, trappers, loggers, and miners. Grinnell championed what amounted to an expansion of Yellowstone's borders through the creation of forest reserves surrounding it. On March 30, 1891, president Benjamin Harrison issued an executive order proclaiming the Yellowstone Park Timberland Reserve, buffering the national park to the south and east with more than a million acres of protected woodlands.

Despite this substantial victory, Grinnell's celebration was short-lived. He was quickly forced to return to the editorial pages of *Forest and Stream* on behalf of Yellowstone yet again. The railroad industry, which had once been the champion of Yellowstone, had transformed into an enemy. The powerful locomotive lobby was working to create a legal right-of-way for the Montana Mineral Railway, which was to cut through the northeast corner of the park including the wildlife-rich Lamar Valley. The line was being pushed by mineral speculators and railroad executives who believed that the small mining town of Cooke City was on the brink of a major gold rush. Grinnell, his cohort of conservationists, and *Forest and Stream* stood firmly against the scheme to "segregate" the northeast corner of the park with the railroad. He railed against the utilitarian arguments made by the railroad lobby, saying "the National Park is founded on sentiment. It is a legislative recognition of the existence in human nature of something higher than the sordid love of gain—than the mere question of dollars and cents."[7]

In 1894, while battling this "segregation scheme," Grinnell dispatched writer Emerson Hough to perform a winter survey of Yellowstone National Park for *Forest and Stream.* Hough's arrival in Yellowstone may be one of the greatest moments of serendipity in American environmental history. Preparing to embark on his wintery expedition with the crude predecessor of cross-country skis, Hough happened to be in the company of Yellowstone's military superintendent, George Anderson. Anderson received a dispatch that an infamous bison poacher, Edgar Howell, had been captured by a park patrol.

A daring and fortuitous turn of events had taken place to bring Edgar Howell into custody. A park patrolman named Felix Burgess and his companion discovered Howell's camp—a teepee and "cache of [bison] heads," strung up in trees to keep them safe from wolves. Shortly after discovering the camp, he heard six shots ring out. Howell was nearby, hunting bison, and "Scout Burgess" engaged in his pursuit.[8] They quickly found Howell busily butchering five freshly slaughtered bison. In order to make the arrest, Burgess had to solve a serious problem: 400 yards of open snow lay between him and Howell. Burgess's only armament was a .38 revolver—no match for the poacher's bison-butchering rifle. Taking his chances, Burgess quickly crossed the open ground. His bravery was met with luck; the brim of Howell's hat shielded his eyes and prevented him from spotting the park patrolman. Fortuitously, the wind blew such that Howell's dog never picked up Burgess's scent. In Burgess's words, "I ran up within 15ft. of Howell, between him and his gun, before I called to him to throw up his hands, and that was the first he knew of anyone but him being anywhere in that country."[9]

The average American would expect the capture of Howell to be an incredible triumph for Yellowstone's protectors and advocates. Surely poaching America's most iconic and endangered animal in its most protected place would result in a serious punishment for Edgar Howell. Emerson Hough's description of Howell's demeanor suggests otherwise, revealing a critical loophole in the protection of Yellowstone: "He was apparently little concerned about his capture... He knew he could not be punished."[10] As Hough later explained, there would be no charges, fines, jail time, community service, or other penalty for such a devious poacher as Edgar Howell. All the park could do to deter him was escort him to the boundary of the park, where their jurisdiction ended. From there he could easily gather new supplies and make another lucrative trip to slaughter America's most iconic megafauna.

Emerson Hough relayed all this information to George Bird Grinnell, who immediately took to the pages of *Forest and Stream*, pushing those in authority to do something about this great miscarriage of justice. Hough joined the military outfit that returned to Howell's camp and retrieved the black-market bison hides and heads. He interviewed Howell, Burgess, and Captain Anderson, writing up the events for a series of articles in *Forest and Stream*. His writing was picked up by numerous other editors across the country. Grinnell accompanied each installment with his own opinions, "determined to wave Howell's bloody knife under the nose of Congress until at last he had closed the legal loophole that endangered the big game for which he had worked so hard to provide sanctuary."[11]

Emerson Hough's reporting and Grinnell's rabble-rousing yielded immediate results. Just three days after Hough's account was published in Grinnell's magazine, Representative John F. Lacey of Iowa introduced a bill to protect Yellowstone's wildlife. The bill gave the Secretary of the Interior the authority to punish individuals like Edgar Howell who committed crimes in a national park. The 1894 Lacey Act stated that "all hunting, or the killing or wounding, or capturing at any time of any bird or wild animal, except dangerous animals, when it is necessary to prevent them from destroying human life or inflicting an injury, is prohibited within the limits of [Yellowstone National Park]," outlining the authority of the Secretary of the Interior to prosecute violations. Poaching a bison, as Howell has done, could now be punished with a fine up to a thousand dollars and two years of prison time. While John Lacey sponsored the bill—part of his own significant legacy in American conservation—credit for the ultimate protection of Yellowstone's wild herds belongs with Emerson Hough and George Bird Grinnell.

While captivated by the natural environment of the American West, Grinnell was also fascinated by the Indigenous people who called it home. A pioneering ethnographer, Grinnell spent months among the Pawnee, Northern Cheyenne, and Blackfeet nations, interviewing their elders and recording their oral traditions. Grinnell's philosophy as a preservationist extended to the Native American cultures that were being swiftly eradicated by white encroachment and forced assimilation. He intended to preserve the rich cultural traditions of the Plains tribes by recording their tribal mythologies and histories, and publishing them as ethnographic anthologies. Because of the time he spent among these tribes, listening to them and never seeking to exploit them, each came to trust him as a valuable ally.

Grinnell's perspective on the Indigenous cultures of the United States is complex. Though he listened to the grievances of the Blackfeet, Cheyenne, and Pawnee, petitioned the government on their behalf, and sought to preserve their cultural heritage, his attitude toward them was ultimately paternalistic. In his mind, he was burdened to help them because they could not help themselves. Grinnell was caught in a self-made paradox, seeking to protect the rich Indigenous cultures that were increasingly endangered while also declaring them hopelessly barbaric and in need of civilization. In one breath, Grinnell both stated the humanity of the Native Americans and declared them savage. Despite his thinly veiled racism and social Darwinism, the Blackfeet trusted Grinnell the most of any white man. For this reason, the Blackfeet requested he join the commission appointed by the Secretary of the Interior to purchase the "mineral strip." They considered him to be their greatest ally—and did not imagine that he could have conflicting interests.

Conflict of Interest at the Crown of the Continent

On September 21, 1895 the Blackfeet offered to sell the mountains in the western half of their reservation to the United States government for two million dollars. This initial offer was rejected by Grinnell and the other commissioners, but the Blackfeet held firm. They believed they had been swindled in previous land deals and that the mountains truly held vast mineral riches, and the leaders of the Blackfeet wanted to be sure that their people received what they were owed. In a second offer, the Blackfeet expanded the land to be sold by approximately one third and asked for three million dollars. Little Dog, a leader of the Blackfeet negotiators, justified their increased price: "There are so many things in which the Great Father has cheated us. Therefore we ask $3,000,000 for that land. Those mountains will never disappear... this money will not last forever."[12] Recognizing that they did not have to purchase the land and believing the mountains held very little gold, copper or oil, Grinnell and the commissioners declared that they would walk away from the negotiations—a response Little Dog predicted. "I knew that you would be afraid when I told you our price."[13]

There was a prevalent idea among the white men involved in the negotiations that the Blackfeet did not care about the mountains.[14] It was believed that in the past the Blackfeet had been a plains culture, living off the bison and seldom using the resources of the Rocky Mountains. In 1895, federal officials viewed the force-assimilated Blackfeet as a cattle-ranching society, further eroding their perceived attachment to the Continental Divide. In reality, the mountains held deep spiritual and practical significance to the Blackfeet. They called them *Mistakis*, the "Backbone of the World." The *Mistakis* was home to a myriad of important spiritual figures including Napi, or Old Man, the creator deity of the Blackfeet. Individual landmarks within the *Mistakis* held their own deep significance, especially Chief Mountain that sits on the border of the park and the reservation. It is "one of the most distinct and spiritually charged land features within the Blackfeet universe."[15]

Though Grinnell and the commission had walked away from negotiations, the Blackfeet still wanted to sell the mineral strip. Inevitably, settlers and prospectors would continue to encroach on and lay claim to the mountains within their reservation; this was their opportunity to receive compensation for the losses that would occur. They convened a meeting among tribal leaders, which included Bureau of Indian Affairs agent George Steell, who had suggested the mineral strip be sold back in 1893. Eager to have the land opened up, Steell convinced the

Blackfeet to accept a lower price.[16] On September 26, 1895, the Blackfeet agreed to sell the mineral strip for one-and-a-half million dollars. The Blackfeet accepted this price on the condition that they could continue to use the natural resources of the Rocky Mountains, outlined by their chief, White Calf: "I want the timber because in the future my children will need it. I also want the grazing land. I would have the right to hunt game and fish in the mountains."[17] These conditions were the lynch-pin of the entire deal. It was crucial for the Blackfeet to maintain these subsistence rights in order to preserve their way of life and stave off starvation.

Throughout the talks, Grinnell appears to behave coldly towards the Blackfeet. He offered them no advice and wrote in his diary that the initial asking price of two million was "absurd."[18] When the Blackfeet increased the price and the amount of land to be sold, Grinnell later described it as "folly." This attitude appears harsh, considering that Grinnell accepted a position on the commission only because "it would be helping the Indians towards self-support and civilization."[19] He held the common belief that the best thing for the Blackfeet (indeed for all Indigenous nations) was to continue assimilating into Euro-American culture.[20] Increased cashflow from selling the mountains would aid that process. But like the Blackfeet, Grinnell also recognized the inevitability of colonial encroachment on the Continental Divide, and saw this as their last chance at compensation for the mountains.

Grinnell told the Blackfeet "we want to see the Indians get as much as possible, but don't want to make fools of them."[21] Informed by his own surveys of the mountains, Grinnell believed they weren't worth the amount the Blackfeet wanted; his attitude in the negotiations was simply honest. He did not believe that Congress would ever approve their asking price and the Blackfeet would be left empty-handed.

A second motivation should also be considered to explain Grinnell's role in the negotiations: his vision of a national park in the region. In 1891, Grinnell had recorded the seed of an idea in his diary: "How would it do to start a movement to buy the St. Mary's country, say 30x30 miles, from the [Blackfeet] Indians at a fair valuation and turn it into a national reservation or park?"[22] Though his energy was focused on defending Yellowstone and its wildlife, Grinnell continued to suggest and develop the idea of a national park in the Northern Rockies throughout the early 1890s. In the spring of 1892, he pitched an article to *The Century Magazine*, intending to describe the "bold" scenery and suggest that "some day it will be a great resort for travelers... within the boundary of one of the proposed forest reserves, and some day I hope may be set aside as a National Park."[23] While journeying back west to Montana in 1894, Grinnell stopped in St. Paul, Minnesota. There, he petitioned the idea to F.J. Whitney, an official with the Great Northern Railroad. "I am anxious to converse with you on the subject of the attractions of the St.

Mary's Lake country and its adaptation for a public park and pleasure resort," he wrote.[24] "The matter is of great interest to me and to other men in the east, and it should be of interest to the intelligent persons of Montana."[25] Though the Blackfeet trusted Grinnell to represent their interests on the commission, he was harboring additional motives, viewing the sale of the Blackfeet land as not only a way for them to receive compensation, but a first step in the process of parkmaking.[26] This sale was an important opportunity for the federal government to take control of this large portion of the Northern Rockies so it could be set aside for a future parkland.

The treaty selling the mineral strip was approved by Congress the following summer, including the stipulations made by White Calf. In April 1898, several hundred eager prospectors rushed into the area, staking out claims for gold, copper, and oil. Small deposits were sporadically discovered, but a lode justifying the price paid for the land was never unearthed. Within five years, the mining boom in the Blackfeet mineral strip was a bust.

George Bird Grinnell was unsurprised that there was no major boom in the ceded strip; he had never believed there was a wealth of mineral resources. By entering the negotiations on the Blackfeet reservation in 1895, Grinnell played a pivotal role in deciding the future of the landscape—and the fate of the Blackfeet. He harbored double motives, laying the groundwork for his vision of a national park while helping the Blackfeet get the most for land that was sure to be slowly stolen away from them. As time would play out, his two motives would prove to be in contradiction with each other. A national park would be established, but its creation would sever the last tether the Blackfeet had to the *Mistakis*.

The Politics of Park-making

By the early 1900s, George Bird Grinnell had begun expanding his campaign to preserve the mountains of the Continental Divide as a national park. As always, *Forest and Stream* was a powerful platform for describing the beauty of the landscape and the qualities worth preserving. Grinnell's conservationist connections included Robert Underwood Johnson, editor of the *Century* and confidant of John Muir, the great defender of Yosemite. In the summer 1901 issue of the *Century*, Grinnell published an editorial titled "The Crown of the Continent." In it, he compared Montana's Northern Rockies to pre-existing parks as a way to argue for their protection: "Here are canons [sic] deeper and narrower than those of the Yellowstone, mountains higher than those of the Yosemite."[27]

While Grinnell used his literary platform effectively, he was ultimately preaching to the choir. His regular readers were already interested in conservation issues and needed little convincing to support a new national park. The individuals Grinnell *did* need to convince resided in the halls of Congress and the state of Montana. He knew that with mineral speculation dwindling, other settlers had already begun to stake claims in the ceded strip. These settlers would undoubtedly oppose land and resources being placed behind the preservation shield of a national park. The residents of northern Montana needed to be convinced that the national park would benefit them—and Congress needed to be convinced that it would benefit the nation.

Despite being well-connected in elite circles, Grinnell was not keen on personally lobbying politicians. He preferred to address political elites under the royal "we" from behind the keys of his typewriter. Luckily, a set of allies joined the Glacier Park campaign who had no problem bringing their influence into the halls of power: James and Louis Hill. Back in 1895, Grinnell had seeded the idea of Glacier National Park when he wrote to the leadership of the Great Northern Railroad on his way to negotiate the mineral strip. Now, that seed was watered by Grinnell's 1901 article in the *Century* and would grow into a robust tendril of influence exactly where Grinnell needed it.

When Grinnell wrote to the Great Northern Railroad, James J. Hill was the president. His son, Louis Hill, took the role 1907 at age 35. Despite there being no evidence of correspondence between the younger Hill and Grinnell, Louis Hill was more preservation-minded than his father and readily took up the cause for Glacier National Park.[28] The Hills and the Great Northern Railroad represented a business interest that had the power to sway both of Grinnell's target audiences. They understood the attitudes and sentiments of resident Montanans, and as the corporation responsible for much of Montana's economic growth—importing new settlers and exporting raw materials—the railroad was a powerful authority on business matters. Because of this, it could credibly dispel fears that "locking up" natural resources in a national park would result in an economic downturn. The Hills enjoyed the influence to make this case to politicians and prospectors alike.

For James and Louis Hill, creating a new national park in Montana—of which their pre-existing railway lines would form the southern border—was much more than just an outgrowth of the conservation zeitgeist. The Hills were aware that their competitor to the south, the Northern Pacific Railway, was successfully profiting off development and tourism in Yellowstone National Park. In the Southwest, the Grand Canyon was proving a popular tourist destination for passengers on the Atchison, Topeka, and Santa Fe Railway. For the Hills, the creation of Glacier National Park represented an opportunity to expand their business into passenger transportation, securing their share of the ever-increasing tourism economy.[29]

For both Grinnell and the Hills, Montana senator Thomas Carter was the first target. He was initially reluctant and uninterested in preservation, believing that America's storehouse of natural resources should be put to use. What the Hills and Grinnell were asking for was wilderness preservation, something industrialists saw as an attempt to "lock up" timber, mineral, and water resources. Despite his apprehension, Carter introduced the first bill to create Glacier National Park in December 1907. The bill promptly failed due to local opposition and Senator Carter did little to revive it. He hoped that perhaps just by introducing the bill, he could satisfy both the Hills and Grinnell. He was wrong.[30]

In February 1908, Carter was pushed by the Hills to begrudgingly introduce new legislation. It quickly moved into the Committee on Public Lands where Montana's second senator, Joseph Dixon, took control of its future. The bill was amended with a compromise: the park boundaries would be extended to include more land, but valid homestead claims and leases within those borders would be allowed to remain. Despite the compromise, Carter remained reluctant to bring the bill to a vote. Grinnell and the Hills had to work aggressively behind the scenes to keep the legislation alive. Both tried to make the case that the park idea was gaining popularity among Montanans. Grinnell went so far as to prod Carter's wife (who had recently visited the Glacier region) to champion the cause with Carter. The Hills worked their congressional connections, pressuring the Speaker of the House, Joseph Cannon, to bring the bill up for a vote.

Because of Carter's lack of urgency, the 1908 bill died with the end of the legislative term. The Hills and Grinnell would not allow this setback to end their dreams of establishing Glacier National Park. Legislation was again introduced in the 1909 session. Grinnell engaged in a flurry of letter writing, working every connection he had in his vast conservation circles. He asked them to write to their representatives in favor of the national park. The Hills continued to build support in Montana, sending bottles of whiskey—labeled "Rocky Boy Elixir of Life"— to prominent locals in order to encourage a favorable opinion of the park project.[31]

As the bill worked its way through Congress in 1909, those inclined to oppose it had two main issues: funding for the park and the potential timber, ore, and agricultural resources that would become off-limits. In debate, several senators expressed concern over the cost of administering a million-acre wilderness area. Proponents of the park bill quickly recognized that it might never pass if it came with a huge initial price tag. It was decided that at its outset Glacier, like Yellowstone, would receive no appropriation from Congress for its establishment and maintenance. The low cost of the park became a fact that Grinnell was quick to point out when lobbying members of Congress. Senator Dixon emphasized in Congressional debate that creating a national park was the best use of the mountains that are "piled up on top of each other."[32] Carter, for his part, emphasized that Glacier could be an economic engine without being logged and timbered. He had previously stated before the Senate, "[T]wo hundred million dollars of the good money of the people of the

United States are paid out annually by Americans visiting the mountains of Switzerland... our people might direct their course to our grand mountains, where scenery equal to that to be found anywhere on the globe may be seen and enjoyed."[33] As the Great Northern Railway knew well, tourism could generate cash almost as well as hitting pay-dirt.

In early 1910, the Glacier Park bill, which had struggled to make headway since 1907, gained momentum. The Senate passed the bill—with amendments allowing inholdings, irrigation projects, and no initial funding—on February 9, 1910. The House of Representatives passed a nearly identical bill on April 29. On May 11, 1910, President William Howard Taft signed the bill establishing Glacier National Park. It was America's tenth national park, stretching across the Continental Divide from the western foothills to the Great Plains.

A Divide of Human Tragedy

The moment President Taft signed the Glacier Park bill, the land changed; in that transformation, it was torn away from the people who knew it since time immemorial. Thousands of miles away, beneath Chief Mountain, the fate of the Blackfeet was decided without their knowledge or intervention. When they had agreed to sell the mineral strip, the Blackfeet were determined to "sell rocks only," keeping their right to hunt, gather, and fish in the mountains.[34] These provisions were so important to the Blackfeet that the deal could not have been made without them. The maintenance of a sliver of their traditional lifeways prevented both the starvation of their people and their culture. The United States government was not blind to the matter. When the Lewis and Clark Forest Reserve was created in 1897, a carve-out was included by President Grover Cleveland clarifying that even with the protective designation, the Blackfeet would maintain their subsistence rights.[35]

No such stipulation was made in the Glacier National Park bill. Unlike the white settlers who kept their inholdings within the park, which included the right to cut mature trees, the Blackfeet weren't considered or mentioned at all in the Glacier legislation. In 1916, government lawyers determined that the subsistence rights of the Blackfeet had been terminated when the park bill was signed into law. Though included in the Lewis and Clark Forest Reserve, the mineral strip was part of the public domain prior to May 11, 1910. As part of the public domain, the federal government could allow citizens to hunt, fish, and cut timber. With the creation of the park, Glacier was withdrawn from the public domain and these activities were banned for the average American. In the eyes of the Interior Department, this ban extended to the Blackfeet, despite their treaty rights. The terms of the 1895 agreement only protected their hunting, gathering, and fishing rights "so long as the [land] shall remain public lands of the United States."[36] To the federal government, Glacier had been withdrawn from the public domain for the purpose of preservation. It was no longer public land—thus the Blackfeet rights expired.

The Blackfeet did not agree with this decision. In their understanding, Glacier was still public land and their rights were reserved by treaty. For the next several decades, a legal—and, at times, nearly physical—war would be waged between the Blackfeet and the National Park Service. At times, the NPS tried to settle the dispute by extending the border for the national park further onto Blackfeet lands. Though the Park Service often cloaked their denial of Blackfeet rights as a wildlife management policy (they didn't want Blackfeet hunting popular fauna enjoyed by tourists such as deer and elk) it worked out in practice as the final dispossession of a people from their homeland. In what could have been a monumental representation of democratic values—a landscape reserved simultaneously for the enjoyment of the American public and the subsistence of its Indigenous people—the park has become a symbol of injustice.[37]

If the story of Glacier National Park is extended a few decades past its founding, the breach of Blackfeet rights becomes a glaring contradiction of what the national park has come to represent. In the summer of 1932, twin laws were passed by the legislatures of Canada and the United States establishing the Waterton-Glacier International

Peace Park. This was a symbolic gesture born out of a desire between citizens of the two nations to remain united amidst the economic and geopolitical anxiety of the Great Depression and interwar Europe. Unlike what had happened to the Blackfeet with the creation of Glacier National Park, there would be no change in the land; it would be managed and understood by the federal government exactly as it had been before. The legislation created Waterton-Glacier International Peace Park in name only, as a decree of "permanent peace and friendship between the two countries."[38] With greater foresight and adherence to democratic principles, Glacier-Waterton could have been proclaimed a peace park for three peoples—a symbolic union between Canada, the United States, and the Indigenous communities that have called the landscapes home since time immemorial.

The story of the creation of Glacier National Park is emblematic of America's early conservation movement, echoing the campaign to create Yellowstone National Park. It has all the proper settings and plots: a passionate elite, a majestic landscape, the threat of privatization, the stolen frontier. George Bird Grinnell saw Montana's Northern Rockies and wanted to see it protected as Yellowstone had been. He believed there was no other practical use for the area and that mining and logging were an active and imminent threat. When considering Grinnell and Glacier, it may be tempting to enshrine them with the ideals with which we now view all national parks: they're uniquely democratic spaces, landscapes preserved and made accessible to present and future generations as a matter of birthright.

In the creation of Glacier National Park, we see a prominent contradiction of these ideals. To create the park, a birthright was revoked. To give the United States a playground, a means of subsistence was cut off. The passion project of one man dispossessed a nation of its homeland. It was declared a peace park, but for more than a century it has represented conflict. Sliced down the middle by the crest of the Rocky Mountains, Glacier National Park preserves the stunning scenery of the Continental Divide; it also enshrines a divide of human tragedy.

GRAND TETON NATIONAL PARK

T HE LANDSCAPE OF GRAND Teton National Park may be one of the most dramatic vistas in all of North America. Stretching out in a long plain, the valley of Jackson Hole is dotted with elk, divided by braided streams and the Snake River. Jackson Lake feeds the Snake as it runs like a moat across the valley, separating the eastern side from the base of the mountains. Like the furred hackles of the wolves that have been restored to Yellowstone in the immediate north, the Teton Range rises from the valley floor in dramatic fashion. A short stack of foothills gives way to the canyons and crags of the granite rampart that shields Jackson Hole to the west. It is scenery from a fantasy world, shadowed by the gun smoke of the Old West.

This was the scenery that captured the life and mind of the writer Struthers Burt. When describing the Tetons in 1924, Burt wrote, "only Maxfield Parrish could paint them, and he makes his mountains up." By his own description, Struthers Burt was an "easterner." He was an academic elite, having graduated from Princeton and studied in Europe. Teaching English at his alma mater, Burt was grabbed by the same wanderlust that gained a chokehold on so many residents of the early 20th century upper crust.

"I cannot remember the time when, at the back of my head, the most fundamental dream of all, there has not been a vision of a small log-house set deep in a pine forest, the sunlight falling in tawny patches through the motionless trees," he wrote. In the summer of 1908, Burt crossed over the "great barrier mountain range that barred the rising sun" as a tourist, hoping a vacation could cure his wanderlust. And so, what began as a holiday transformed into a lifetime of advocacy for protecting the wild places that made his heart full.[1]

Burt's accommodations in Jackson Hole, Wyoming, were at the JY Ranch. It served as a home base for rambles in the wilderness and hunting pronghorns. Burt was so enchanted by the ranch and the surrounding scenery that he found himself scraping together the funds to purchase an option on a half-stake in its ownership. This put him into business with Louis Joy, a visionary entrepreneur but toxic partner who would kickstart a new tourism industry in Jackson Hole.

By the time Burt purchased his share in the JY Ranch, it was becoming clear that cattle-ranching in the highland valley was a bust. Homesteading laws limited settlers to improving and claiming 160 acres of land—enough for a decent living, but only if the American West were as verdant and fertile as the lands east of the Mississippi River. Unfortunately for many who braved the perilous journey west from St. Louis, the western territories were considerably drier than they imagined.

The landscape beyond the 100th meridian had been termed "the Arid West" by John Wesley Powell, the first chief of the U.S. Geological Survey.[2] The lack of water made traditional agriculture a fruitless effort. Ranging cattle was a reasonable alternative, but 160 acres wasn't nearly enough for a small herd of one hundred head. A hardy settler could double his holding by filing a desert land claim, but that required the back-breaking work of constructing irrigation to become valid.

Add adverse economic conditions, and many Jackson Hole settlers gave up on cattle-ranching after the turn of the 20th century. In order to buoy their finances, they began taking in tourists who had been drawn by the rugged beauty of the Teton Range and the Snake River—tourists like Struthers Burt. These tourists were called "dudes." In Burt's popular pseudo-memoir *Diary of a Dude Wrangler*, he explains that, "The word [dude] has none of the slurring connotations attached to the term tenderfoot. It does not imply ignorance or softness, it simply means someone, usually a person not resident in the country, who hires someone else to guide him or cook for him, or who pays money to stay on a ranch. The governor of Wyoming can be a dude if he hires guides when he goes hunting, so can the oldest and toughest cattleman in the world."

Put simply, a dude was a tourist who was attracted to a more rustic pageantry. The dude-ranching industry materialized toward the end of the 19th century, at a time when the romance of the Old West was fading and the American frontier had been declared closed. Dudes longed to reach back to that time, stepping into a vignette of recent history that was equal parts cowboy caricature and homemade hospitality. They wanted to hunt and ride, drink gritty coffee, take in the majesty of the mountains, and they didn't want to wear a tie at dinner. But they also wanted to know that there *would be dinner*, well-prepared by another's labor and with dessert to follow. As Struthers Burt wrote, "[it's] giving people home-made bedsteads but forty-pound mattresses."[3]

When Struthers Burt came to the JY Ranch in 1908, he was the epitome of a dude. He was young and of means, well-connected and well-educated. In the eyes of Louis Joy, Burt was the perfect person to advertise the JY to like-minded individuals in the East. Joy was shrewd enough to know that his property was both blessed and cursed by the environment. The soil was too thin for crops and the grass too crabby for livestock, but the JY "consisted of a hundred and sixty acres of timbered land lying along a lake at the base of the Tetons... it had, and still has, one of the most superb views in the Rockies, a view that even my juvenile instinct told me someday might be worth a fortune."[4] For this reason, Struthers Burt entered the business. He was utterly cashless, but he undertook the metamorphosis from dude to dude wrangler nonetheless.

The Rugged Country Beneath the Tetons

As the settlers of the late 19th century discovered, it has always taken a particularly strong-willed individual to make a home in—or even a trip to—Jackson Hole. Because of that, John Colter receives a second jewel in the crown of western mythology, being the first to traverse not only the Yellowstone Plateau but also Jackson Hole. Colter takes credit as the first Euro-American to take in the majesty of the Tetons. However, like his circuitous route through Yellowstone, the record of Colter's trek through Jackson Hole can be dubious at best. The evidence in his favor is a poorly drawn map and an inscribed rock, cemented together by decades of storytelling.

According to legend, Colter trekked south through the valley of the Snake River, crossed the Tetons, and looped back north through the Teton Basin. He would have sheltered during the worst of the 1808-1809 winter—which was almost certainly harsh, dark and lonely—around the Teton range before circling back through Yellowstone. Once again, the lack of a direct account or consistent map from Colter casts doubt on his accomplishment.

Fortunately for John Colter's legacy, there is evidence to corroborate the shaky story told by the map. In 1931 a farmer named William Beard discovered a block of hardened lava, about the size of a basketball, that appears to be inscribed with the words "John Colter 1808." Beard lived on the western side of the Teton Range, just inside the Wyoming border. It is highly likely that Colter would have spent the winter there, making the etched date of 1808 accurate. In 1933, a neighbor acquired the "Colter Stone" in exchange for a pair of boots, and donated it to the National Park Service. Park geologists have confirmed that the weathering on the rhyolite block is consistent with the dating. Taken together—and considered in light of his epic odyssey through Yellowstone—the map and Colter Stone point towards a potential second incredible achievement for the mountain man. He is a fascinating character who was at the launch of (for Euro-Americans) the long history of two incredibly popular parks.[5]

While he was likely the first, Colter was certainly not the last mountain man to trek through Jackson Hole. The Tetons became an important landmark for Rocky Mountain fur trappers, at one time referred to as the "Pilot Knobs." Their modern name comes from the homesick imagination of French fur trappers, worked up after many solitary months in the bush: *Trois Tetons* translates to "three breasts."[6] As trappers worked the many major rivers that converged in the vicinity of the range, their distinct shape and dramatic uplift served as an important navigation tool.

In 1859, the famous fur trapper Jim Bridger was hired to guide a military reconnaissance of the region, serving as pathfinder for the expedition of Captain William F. Raynolds. Raynolds's mission was to survey both the landscape and its inhabitants, determining the suitability and safety for roads and railways in the region. Raynolds's party was accompanied by a young Ferdinand Vanderveer Hayden. Just as he would be in future expeditions (and as the future head of the U.S. Geological Survey of the Territories), Hayden was completely occupied by opportunities for discovery. At times impatient, he would detach himself from the main party to investigate irregularities in the terrain, annoying his companions and delaying their progress.[7]

A chief aim of the Raynolds Expedition was to travel up the Yellowstone River and into the highlands. If they had succeeded, they would have been the first scientific expedition into the future park, predating the Folsom Party by a decade. Unfortunately, heavy snowfall blocked their route and confused their guide, preventing them from finding a pass onto the Yellowstone Plateau. Instead, they were forced toward Jackson Hole, leaving Yellowstone *terra incognita* for several more years.[8]

For more than a decade after Raynolds, little passed beneath the Tetons but elk and antelope. With the establishment of America's first national park to the north in 1872, the mystery of the region was beginning to be dispelled. Military officers conducted additional surveys of the region around Yellowstone. In 1873, Captain William Jones found a suitable route for a road through Togwhotee Pass, though none was built in that time. In 1876, Lieutenant Gustavus Doane (who had provided escort for the 1870 Washburn Expedition into Yellowstone) embarked on a survey of the Snake River. Doane must have underestimated the brutal winter conditions that the Teton Range could produce, embarking on his expedition in the early autumn. His men suffered as a result. Heavy snowfall made their progress slow, putting strain on their rations. When their boat capsized in the rough waters of the Snake River, his men nearly froze to death. Their fortuitous discovery of a fur trapper's cabin was the only thing that prevented a disaster and an end to their journey.

After his highly successful survey of Yellowstone in 1871, Ferdinand Hayden received a second appropriation from Congress to fund his U.S. Geological and Geographical Survey of the Territories. The Survey had similar goals to his 1871 expedition, but this time was split into two divisions. One, led by Hayden, would continue to chart and document the resources of the Yellowstone Plateau. The second, led by James Stevenson, was tasked with surveying the Snake River. This expedition was populated by many of the same men who had helped establish Yellowstone National Park, further solidifying their place as important individuals in the history of the American West.

Like the Yellowstone Expedition, Hayden staffed his crew with a range of scientists and professionals, including the photographer William Henry Jackson. This time Jackson was assigned to join the Snake River Division in a "country hitherto unphotographed."[9] In many of Jackson's photos, the three Tetons are seen through the frame of other land forms. They edge between the hills, as though tempting the viewer to come closer and see the peaks for themselves.

Nathaniel Pitt Langford, serving as superintendent of Yellowstone Park at the time, joined the Snake River Division "as a guest."[10] While Langford made detailed comments in his report on the suitability of the region for stock-raising and railroad development, it would seem that his primary objective was to summit the highest and most prominent peak in the Teton Range. Alongside expedition leader James Stevenson, Langford became the first white man to summit the Grand Teton. Writing about the difficulty of the ascent, he said, "at one or two points when nearing the summit we would have been obliged to abandon the task but for the aid we received by casting a rope over prominent projections and pulling ourselves over them, to places where we could obtain secure footholds. In one of these efforts Mr. Stevenson came near losing his hold and falling down a precipice nearly a thousand feet."[11]

The Tetons in the hazy distance, 1872, William Henry Jackson. Courtesy NPS History Collection.

Each party of Teton explorers faced similar circumstances produced by the geography of Jackson Hole. Foremost was the rough and rugged nature of the landscape. Even in the early summer, the high passes and heavy snowfall were treacherous enough to prevent Captain Raynolds from being able to reach his true objective, which was Yellowstone. It was similar conditions that may have left John Colter feeling trapped in his 1808 winter bivouac, carving his name in a rock to "while away the time" and stave off loneliness.[12] A December attempt at running the Snake River was nearly the end of the Doane expedition. Across the decades, each set of explorers found that the jagged, canine peaks of the three Tetons were an omen, a foreshadowing of just how treacherous the terrain could be.

But a second shared experience was the incredible beauty of the landscape. As each successive wave of exploration took in the scenery for the first time, they filled their records with praise for its picturesque quality. As if describing the gates of Heaven, Captain Raynolds wrote, "Far off, a barrier apparently stretched across the valley in the form of a ragged cliff of brilliant red, above whose centre [sic] shone with even greater brilliancy the snow-covered peaks of the Great Teton, dazzling in the clear atmosphere, with the reflected rays of the newly-risen sun."[13] More than a decade later, William Henry Jackson wrote that upon climbing to a high vantage point, "we were rewarded with one of the most stupendous panoramas in all of America."[14]

These men, spread across nearly a century, took in the evidence to reach the same conclusion that Struthers Burt and many others would reach. The greatest resource of Jackson Hole wasn't its fertile soil or rangeland. Rather, it possessed a simpler, more elusive potential. The true value of the Grand Tetons was their grandeur and modern man's desire to dwell in their shadow. Struthers Burt and Louis Joy came to this conclusion in 1908. It was a conclusion that would come to shape the history of the valley in all its facets.

"War" in Jackson Hole

Though the time would come when the landscape itself would be the object of preservationist zeal, early actions centered on protection of the wild elk herds. The majestic antlered ungulates ranged across the Northern Rocky Mountains, migrating to lower elevations in the winter. With traditional cattle ranching having proved too difficult to manage, elk represented a multi-faceted economic resource that kept many settlers afloat. Primarily, elk were a source of food; a single animal could represent hundreds of pounds of meat. Their antlers also made handsome trophies, drawing dudes from the east with plenty of cash to the spare rooms of settlers willing to accommodate them. Hospitality was readily available among homesteaders who could supplement their thinly stretched incomes guiding hunters in search of elk heads.

However, reliance on the elk became problematic for settlers when the herds began to decline in the 1890s. Seeking an explanation for the unfolding tragedy, the residents of Jackson Hole found scapegoats. A lineup of classic Wild West criminals was established, ranging from wolves to poachers to Indigenous populations. While predators were exterminated and poachers punished, it was the Bannock and Shoshone that suffered most from the ire of white pioneers.

Like in Yellowstone, Indigenous people had been taking advantage of the natural resources seasonally afforded by the landscape for thousands of years before the arrival of white settlers. In fact, the range of Yellowstone's Sheepeater Shoshone extended south into the Teton range. Like Struthers Burt who arrived decades later, the Shoshone understood the jagged peaks with awe and reverence. Indeed, they experienced the landscape as more than just aesthetically beautiful, but also spiritually significant. Mountain peaks represented gateways to the spirit world. Semicircular stone formations found in the high alpine areas demonstrate that Indigenous people ascended the high tower of the Tetons seeking help from the spirit world to aid them in hunting and healing.[15] One such stone circle was discovered and described by Nathaniel Pitt Langford and Alexander Stevenson upon their ascent of the Grand Teton—making them the first white men to ever crest the peak.

Like the Blackfeet, the Shoshone and Bannock tribes signed a treaty in 1864 establishing a massive reservation stretching across modern-day Wyoming, Utah, Idaho, and Nevada. Within just a few years, the reservation was reduced and split apart by the 1868 Treaty of Fort Bridger. Similar to the 1895 Blackfeet Agreement, the Fort Bridger Treaty reserved hunting rights for the tribes, made available to them on vast unoccupied tracts of the public d omain.[16] Just as it was for the Jackson Hole settlers, the right to hunt was a practical necessity for the survival of the Indigenous communities. With the arrival of white homesteaders in 1884 and decline of the elk herds in the 1890s, this right would prove contentious—and lead to a violent bid to drive out the Bannock and Shoshone.

As tribal hunting parties entered public land around Jackson Hole, taking elk for their own survival, they were thought of by Jackson Hole settlers as wasteful lawbreakers. The shrinking herds were *their* fault. Despite their treaty rights permitting it, white settlers claimed that the Indigenous hunters broke state game laws by taking elk year-round. The pioneers took the law into their own hands. A Jackson Hole constable deputized locals and began arresting Bannock hunters in 1895, fining them and confiscating their elk hides.

By midsummer 1895, frustration and prejudice among white settlers reached a boiling point. When deputies encountered Bannock hunting party in the Gros Ventre range on June 30, a posse was formed to punish the hunters for alleged crimes committed—namely, violating the state game laws that their federal treaty rights superseded. The frenzied mob succeeded in arresting several Bannock. When the prisoners and their captors entered a dense grove of trees on the way to the jail, the deputies produced loaded rifles.[17] Fearing they were about to be murdered, the Bannock panicked and scattered into the forest. Shots rang out. The elderly, half-blind man Se-we-a-gat was shot four times in the back and perished. A younger man, Nemuts, was shot twice but recovered. With the clamoring of rifles in white settler hands, the Bannock "War" of 1895 had begun.

Attempting to blame the violence on the victims, Jackson Hole settlers sent out reports that the innocent settlers had been threatened by the savage Bannock. Those reports echoed around the nation, widely repeated in eastern newspapers—but those reverberations soon rang hollow. It didn't take much investigation for the reality of the situation (that the white settlers were the instigators of the conflict) to be revealed. In August 1895, the Chicago Tribune wrote, "The latest authentic report from Jackson's Hole [sic] is to the effect ... that the Bannocks, off their reservation, are peaceable and trying to get back; and that the only danger is that white settlers may attack and murder them before they are again under government protection, and this is all there is to the Bannock war."[18]

A New York publication echoed the sentiment, saying, "it looks as if the white settlers had determined to turn a peaceable hunting expedition into a race war."[19]

The settler-sparked Bannock War prompted federal officials to seek a clarification of Bannock and Shoshone hunting rights. A test case was staged in which two Bannock hunters were charged with breaking Wyoming state game laws. It became *Ward v. Race Horse*. Central to the case was the question of which had the greater legal authority: the 1868 treaty, ratified by Congress while Wyoming was yet a territory, or the recent game laws passed by the state of Wyoming after entering the Union.

In a seven-to-one vote, the Supreme Court sided with the State of Wyoming. Only Justice Henry Billings Brown dissented—the same Justice who would write the majority opinion for *Plessy v. Ferguson* one week later, codifying the "separate but equal" doctrine. They determined that while the *territory* of Wyoming had been required to honor the treaty, the new *state* of Wyoming was not. Additionally, they ruled that Congress could limit the treaty terms as it pleased. The Court cited the establishment of Yellowstone National Park and the 1894 Lacey Act protecting Yellowstone bison as examples of Congress limiting Indigenous hunting rights outside of their reservations.[20]

The single dissent in the decision hinged on one of the traditional methods of interpreting treaties with Native American tribes: that they must be interpreted as the tribe would have understood them when the treaty was signed.

In 1868, the Bannock and Shoshone would have taken the terms of the treaty to mean that they held their hunting rights in perpetuity. Just as the Blackfeet could not have predicted how the creation of a national park would affect their subsistence rights decades later, the Bannock and Shoshone could not have predicted the creation of the state of Wyoming in 1890 and its subsequent game laws that would limit their rights.

With the decision of *Ward v. Racehorse* in favor of the State of Wyoming, the residents of Jackson Hole saw their great scheme completed. The conflict they sparked had the effect of safeguarding *their* elk from Indigenous hunters. Though two Bannock had been murdered, the settlers suffered no legal penalty; in fact, their actions were implicitly affirmed by the Supreme Court ruling. Like *Plessy v. Ferguson*, it was later determined that the Supreme Court had been incorrect in its 1896 ruling. *Ward v. Racehorse* was overturned by the 2019 case, *Herrera v. Wyoming*. In a 5-4 decision, the Supreme Court determined that the admission of Wyoming as a state did not, in fact, undo the treaty rights established by Congress in 1868.

The Forest Reserves

The result of the Bannock War of 1895 was just one way in which broader cultural movements expressed themselves in Wyoming's remote northwest. The broken treaty and ultimate dispossession of the Bannock and Shoshone is reminiscent of the Blackfeet east of the Continental Divide—along with countless other interactions between tribes and the federal government at the turn of the 20th century. In an era of Indian boarding schools in the east, Indian Wars across the territories, and the passage of the Dawes Act in 1887 (which allowed white settlers to encroach further onto reservation lands) *Ward v. Race Horse* was just one expression of a broader trend.

Similarly, a growing sentiment for the preservation of landscapes swirled in the American atmosphere. It is a sentiment that the Jackson Hole pioneers felt instinctually as the elk disappeared and one that cannot be disconnected from the simultaneous erasure of Native Americans both from the landscape and from memory. To white Americans, the geographies that most deserved to be set aside were the most remote and rugged, vignettes of wilderness to be protected from the encroachment of industry. The concept of wilderness precludes the presence of mankind and their civilizing tendencies. In this mythology, any trace of humanity native to the landscape must either be expelled or reduced to savagery.

In 1890, the concept of the national park as a landscape preservation tool began to solidify with the establishment of Yosemite and Sequoia national parks in their original, albeit limited, forms. The following year, one of the most important conservation laws in American history passed Congress "with virtually no opposition."[21] It was the Forest Reserve Act, a bill written in direct response to the rapidly diminishing natural resources of the west. Like the Lacey Act that would follow a few years later, the 1891 Forest Reserve Act represented a shift in American thought surrounding natural resources; that they were not infinite, and that some portions should be reserved for future generations. From bison to redwoods, the natural wonders of the west were being decimated by development and industry. Pressure was building to save them, and the Forest Reserve Act was one of the earliest valve releases.

Using the power of the Forest Reserve Act, which allowed the president to place tracts of forest land in the public domain inside reserves, President Benjamin Harrison issued a proclamation that would bring the forces of conservation within eyeshot of the Tetons for the first time. The 1.2 million-acre Yellowstone Park Timber Reserve was created by presidential decree, stretching south from the park border toward the mountain range. Over the next decade, this initial forest reserve would morph and evolve, its name and borders shifting and expanding. In 1897, President Grover Cleveland extended protections with the establishment of the Teton Forest Reserve, which covered much of present-day Grand Teton National Park.

To the Jackson Hole pioneers, this proclamation-based introduction of federal oversight felt heavy-handed. It wasn't taken lightly. A 1902 article in *The*

Billings Gazette titled "Obnoxious Laws" states "there is trouble brewing down in northern Wyoming and trouble of the most serious kind. Ever since the president... issued his proclamation extending the forest reservation along the east side of the Yellowstone park [sic]."[22] The drawing of borders and establishment of government jurisdiction meant rules: regulations for grazing allotments, boundaries, permits, and fees. These realities rubbed raw against the frontier spirit that so many of the settlers embodied, resulting in resistance.

Eventually, settlers began to recognize the benefits offered by the presence of the U.S. Forest Service. Though remote, Jackson Hole and the surrounding mountain ranges were not impervious to a Tragedy of the Commons—the economic concept that shared resources would be rapidly depleted if not carefully managed for the long term. As always, the state of the Jackson Hole elk herd was the most prominent pain point. The U.S. Forest Service represented a force that could improve their plight, driving out poachers who slaughtered elk for their eyeeteeth. Termed "tuskers," the intrusion of these poachers threatened the very survival of the regional herds as they slaughtered a huge number of elk and left the corpses to rot while harvesting only their ivory. In addition, the Forest Service enhanced infrastructure by building roads, trails, and telephone lines, and hired many of the locals to complete these projects.[23]

Though Yellowstone National Park was created to the north of Jackson Hole before pioneers ever arrived there, the proclamation of the forest reserves was the first significant experience they had with federal land management. Over the coming decades, the presence of federal land agencies would only grow in the shadow of the Tetons. As they did, the arrival of the forest reserves birthed a pattern for how residents of the valley would relate to increased oversight. Initially there would be hesitation—perhaps even hostility. Eventually, when the prophesied benefits of regulation came true, there would be acceptance. When faced with an existential threat, such as the loss of the elk herds that supported their livelihoods, there would ultimately be cooperation and mutual benefit between the settlers and the federal government.

The Elk Park

Around the turn of the 20th century, the plight of the elk herds did not meaningfully change. Their decline continued, driving the first tangible moves toward preservation beneath the Tetons. As early as 1882, General Phillip Sheridan suggested extending the boundary of Yellowstone National Park forty miles south, so as to encompass a broader expanse of elk habitat. In 1897, the military superintendent of Yellowstone lamented tusker activity outside of the park's boundaries, where he had no authority to address it. In 1898, the director of the U.S. Geological Survey, Charles Walcott, echoed the sentiment, suggesting a new and expansive Teton National Park to take in large swathes of forest and mountain south of Yellowstone.[24]

Each of these suggestions was followed by inaction. No one with the authority to act would pursue national park status for the Tetons and Jackson Hole until 1915. Despite this, the elk ranging between the Yellowstone uplands and Jackson Hole were still perceived to be in a serious predicament—and serious action should be taken on their behalf.

Trouble for the elk continued to center around "that historic pageant of animal migration ... the annual travel of the elk from their summer pastures around the headwaters of the Snake River and the upper Yellowstone River to the valley lands of Jackson Hole."[25] In order to reach this range, the elk were forced to traverse the homesteads and settlements of Jackson Hole residents, causing chaos—and, in many cases, horror. Desperately searching for winter forage, the elk found much of their normal range was already grazed over by livestock or bound up by barbed wire fences. Fighting to survive the harsh Teton winters, the elk prosecuted a campaign against mankind's impositions over their ancient migration paths. The elk devoured haystacks, ripped down fences, and trampled through homesteads. Despite these pitched attempts at survival, thousands of elk languished and starved, littering the landscape with their corpses.

Though the elk stole their cattle feed and destroyed their property, the pioneers took pity on them. The winter of 1908-1909 was particularly severe and resulted in a massive die-off. It was an ecological tragedy—and a turning point. That year the state of Wyoming contributed funds to purchase hay for the starving ungulates and requested land be set aside for an elk refuge. Stephen Leek, a community leader and photographer, documented the season of desperation. He published images of starving and frozen elk in outdoors magazines and toured them throughout Western states. These efforts publicized the issue and built sympathy for the charismatic megafauna, which were considered by many to be a disappearing icon of the old rugged West.

In 1912, the National Elk Refuge was created to protect the winter range of the migrating herds north of the town of Jackson, within the valley of Jackson Hole. To create the refuge, Congress appropriated funds to purchase ranchlands and withdrew land in the public domain. To prevent elk from raiding haystacks intended for livestock, a feeding program was implemented on the refuge. This would become a repeating pattern beneath the Tetons: faced with an existential threat in the decline of the elk, the residents of Jackson Hole supported the use of the public domain and public policy to protect their natural resources. Contrasting with the Forest Service policy of *using* the public domain for grazing or timber harvesting, the creation of the elk refuge was a step toward *reserving* the land for the benefit of the elk.

Though imperfect (the policy of providing the elk with supplementary winter feed is controversial among wildlife biologists), the creation of the National Elk Refuge represents the first step toward preservation in Jackson Hole. While it would be easy to think that protection of the elk was altruistic, it was ultimately for the benefit of the settlers. Though we often conceive of preservation as being oriented toward the wellbeing of landscapes and wildlife, we must remember that there are a variety of motivations that contribute to protective designations such as wildlife refuges or national parks. For the residents of Jackson Hole, the value of the elk was multi-faceted; they relied on them for daily subsistence, as well as to draw in dudes and their overstuffed wallets.

Unlike in Yellowstone to the north, the growing forces of preservation in the valley would continue to follow this line—increased protections not for the sake of the landscape, but for the sake of the people who valued it. Because of that thinking, a transition can be seen from the establishment of Yellowstone National Park to the creation of a park in Jackson Hole. In 1872, the borders were drawn around the geothermal features to prevent human abuse of their scenic value; in the Tetons, the park would serve to enshrine the ways mankind was already interacting with the landscape.

Enter Horace Albright

While early observers of the Tetons and Jackson Hole had noted its worthiness as a national park, no serious movement toward the idea would be made until 1915. In the summer of that year, Stephen Mather, a mining-made millionaire, was engaged in a frenzied campaign to establish a federal bureau to manage the rapidly expanding national park system. He was aided by Horace Albright, a freshly-graduated law student from California. Together the two men would shape the policies, practices, and expansion of the National Park Service. For his part, Horace Albright would leave his greatest legacy in the Tetons.

In those early years Mather and Albright spent a great deal of time cozying up to politicians, dignitaries, business, and media men, always seeking support for national parks in both urban halls of power and the rugged backcountry. Though this strategy was largely successful—coupled with a media blitz to better acquaint the public with their national parks—momentum stalled after the bill to create the National Park Service passed the House of Representatives. Restless and eager to see their project through, Mather arranged a visit to Yellowstone National Park for Assistant Attorney General Huston Thompson and his wife. Perhaps their endorsement of the Park Service bill could get the ball rolling once again.

Yellowstone Superintendent Horace Albright, 1919. Courtesy of NPS History Collection.

While touring a newly constructed road between the national park and Jackson Lake, Mather, Albright, and their guests took in two sights that would portend the future of the National Park Service in the region. The first was Jackson Lake itself: an artificial reservoir constructed by the Bureau of Reclamation, drowning thousands of acres of the Teton National Forest. "The Reclamation people had not cleared out the trees before flooding the area, and it made a very ugly sight," wrote Albright.[26] As he would discover in just a few years, the ugly sight of a landscape ruined by "reclamation" would be a strange gift.

As they continued southward, "these disturbing sights were almost forgotten." Albright was approaching the Tetons and Jackson Hole—and it was going to impress him in a way that no other landscape had:

"It was the first time Mather and I had ever seen the spectacular panorama of the Grand Teton mountain range from the lowlands of the Snake River Valley. I had never beheld such scenery. I knew the Sierra Nevada and had climbed Mount Whitney, but here before us were the Alps of America. Mather and I were both flabbergasted, and we agreed that this whole magnificent area ought to be added to Yellowstone National Park."[27]

By the end of that summer, the National Park Service was established. Shortly thereafter, Stephen Mather was appointed as its first director and Horace Albright as his assistant director. In preparing their first annual report to the Secretary of the Interior on the state of the National

Park Service, Albright recalled the experience of taking in the alpine scenery for the first time. Centering his report on seven major objectives for the budding agency, he included the acquisition of the Tetons.

On May 13, 1918, Albright reiterated the importance of acquiring the Tetons and Jackson Hole for the National Park System in a 23-point letter to Interior Secretary Franklin Lane. This letter, which was circulated among prominent conservationists and approved by Stephen Mather, was considered "A Creed for the Parks," guiding their development on both a philosophical and practical level. As such, Albright tied his desire to gain the Tetons to a guiding principle for the young Park Service:

"You should study existing national parks with the idea of improving them by the addition of adjacent areas which will complete their scenic purposes or facilitate administration. The addition of the Teton Mountains to the Yellowstone National Park, for instance, will supply Yellowstone's greatest need, which is an uplift of glacier-bearing peaks; and the addition to the Sequoia National Park of the Sierra summits and slopes to the north and east, as contemplated by pending legislation, will create a reservation unique in the world, because of its combination of gigantic trees, extraordinary canyons, and mountain masses."[28]

As far as Horace Albright was concerned, the stage was set for the Teton Range to join the national park system. Including it as an extension of Yellowstone was simpler and easier to manage than creating a whole new national park. More than just an item on his personal wish list, Albright was able to tie the acquisition to the fundamental principles being developed for the pioneering agency. From his lofty perspective on the Yellowstone plateau, it probably seemed like one of his easier objectives to accomplish.

He was sorely mistaken.

Dude Riling

In April 1918, Wyoming Representative Frank Mondell introduced a bill to extend Yellowstone National Park southward. The new boundaries would include the Teton Range, Jackson Lake, and the naturally formed lakes at the foot of the mountains. In February 1919, a version of the bill passed unanimously in the House of Representatives. In these early years of the National Park Service, the agency received broad support and the enthusiasm for park-making was almost tangible. In preparation for the park extension, President Woodrow Wilson withdrew a large tract of the Teton National Forest from the public domain, ready to be preserved as parkland. Believing that every detail was sorted and every necessary endorsement signed off, Horace Albright sat on the cusp of achieving one of his most important policy goals: adding the Grand Teton landscape to the National Park Service.

However, he was jolted from this pleasant daydream. At the last minute, Idaho Senator John Nugent was persuaded by local livestock interests—sheepmen in particular—to oppose the park extension. With the Senate in filibuster, Nugent's opposition vote single-handedly killed the bill and effectively halted the creation of a national park in the region for a decade.

Though Horace Albright had gained the approval of a significant set of politicians, including the congressmen and governor of Wyoming, he had failed to consult a key constituency: the residents of Jackson Hole. This became glaringly obvious when Albright attended a public meeting in Jackson Hole, intending to kickstart renewed support for the Yellowstone extension. Walking into the meeting blind, Albright pitched the promises of a national park that usually garnered enthusiastic support: new roads and tourist dollars. He quickly discovered that Old West individualism hung as thick in the air as cigarette smoke. "The idea was a red flag," he later recounted "[to] the ranchers and dude ranchers, who saw it as a forerunner of federal interference and as the opening wedge in bringing unwanted development."[29]

Struthers Burt—who successfully owned and operated the Bar BC dude ranch by this point—was present at the meeting with his business partner, Horace Carncross. In a published exchange with Congressman Frank Mondell, he explained the reasons he and other locals opposed the park extension. "I have been in Yellowstone park many times, but never without undergoing disagreeable experiences, and without coming away with a most unfavorable impression," he wrote in the *Jackson Hole Courier*.[30]

Burt addressed each argument in favor of the Yellowstone extension individually, using his professional writer's prose to crisply slap down each in turn. New roads? The Forest Service already represented federal control in the area and was constructing decent enough travel corridors on its own. Increased tourism? The true beneficiaries would be the Yellowstone hotels and guides, who could charge more money for longer trips into Jackson Hole, crowding out the smaller dude ranchers. Protecting the elk? "The preservation of the game is entirely dependent upon winter conditions," he asserted. "At present the elk are doing splendidly, and will continue to do so as long as they are fed."

With the practical argument made by the NPS dismantled, Burt turned his pen to the agency's central philosophy. "It seems to me, therefore, that you have brought forward no argument except those based on sentiment, and although I would be the last to oppose arguments of that kind, in my opinion, they are the very worst you could use." Struthers Burt understood the real reason Albright had his sights set on Jackson Hole and the Tetons: the landscape was a scenic jewel in the diadem of the West.

Burt agreed with Albright entirely—it was, after all, the beauty of the landscape that had uprooted him from an eastern professorship and landed him in the dude-wrangling business. However, based on his experiences with Yellowstone to the north, Burt didn't believe that the NPS could serve Jackson Hole anything that was not already on the table. He believed that the Park Service—in particular its protective regulations and gawking tourists—posed an existential threat to the valley. "Jackson Hole is eminently a 'people's playground,'" he wrote. "It is growing every year; growing naturally. Under the wise rule of the forest service [sic], the people actually do 'play,' and at the same time the beauty and natural resources of the country are entirely conserved... To render this country similar to Yellowstone park; in other words, you propose to make it a dust heap, pyramid it with carefully collected tin cans, put signs all over it, and herd whoever visits it around as livestock is herded."

With the defeat of the Yellowstone extension and local sentiment placed in firm opposition, Horace Albright resigned to the fact that he would have to "bide [his] time and eventually find ways to win the [local's] support." As Burt outlined in his letter to Representative Mondell, the ranchers and dude wranglers of the valley saw no benefit to introducing new government oversight. They were reluctantly satisfied with the work of the U.S. Forest Service and had no interest in allowing the dual mission of the National Park Service to introduce both higher standards of landscape protection and blissfully naive crowds of tourists. For Struthers Burt and his neighbors, there was simply no practical, personal benefit in bringing Yellowstone south.

Damming Jackson Hole

Despite this initial setback, Horace Albright set out on a slow-burning campaign to bring Jackson Hole under National Park Service jurisdiction. After becoming superintendent of Yellowstone in 1919, he was well-positioned to stay involved in the valley. When people of influence visited Yellowstone, Albright always planned an excursion to the south side of the park. From there, he'd take them in eye-shot of the *Trois Tetons*, hinting at how wonderful they'd be as an extended feature of the nation's first wilderness parkland. Albright employed this strategy on a variety of cultural and political elites. Even President Warren G. Harding was persuaded to support the park extension in 1923. It will never be known what his endorsement could have meant, as he fell ill and died just a few weeks later.

While endorsements from elites were encouraging, they were not what Albright needed to see his dream fulfilled—he needed Struthers Burt and the dude wranglers on his side. In a stroke of bureaucratic good fortune, the National Park Service already possessed the necessary tool for demonstrating an alignment of interests to the prominent citizens of Jackson Hole. Back when the passage of the Yellowstone extension bill seemed imminent, President Woodrow Wilson withdrew 600,000 acres of the Teton National Forest from settlement. The National Park Service was given the right of first review, a power that gave them the authority to block any proposed development. They wielded the power judiciously.

Through this authority, the National Park Service was able to block the construction of multiple dams at the outlet of the lakes lying at the base of the Tetons. As was already well known by preservationists—and would be continuously confirmed over the next several decades—water storage projects had a unique power to destroy scenic resources.[31] The construction of a dam where the Snake River flowed out of Jackson Lake in 1906 had raised the water level, drowning a huge tract of surrounding forest and creating an ugly and destitute sight that Horace Albright and Stephen Mather had witnessed during their first visit to Jackson Hole in 1915. When dams were proposed to raise the level of Jenny and Leigh lakes, the National Park Service vetoed them. Doubling down, a second water storage scheme was prevented at Emma Matilda and Two Ocean lakes, which were deemed "less scenic" and thus better suited to be irreparably altered by inundation.[32]

This display of bureaucratic force by the Park Service produced three effects. The first was the preservation of the landscape. If Albright's ambitions were to be fulfilled, permanent degradation of natural resources had to be stalled. Woodrow Wilson's 1918 withdrawal gave the NPS the exact tool needed to do so.

Second, the U.S. Forest Service and National Park Service were placed in direct opposition. Already tensions had brewed between the USFS and NPS over which agency would be a better steward of the nation's scenery and natural resources. Though being swiftly eclipsed by the Park Service in terms of recreation and preservation, the Forest Service made the case that they were just as capable and qualified to meet these ends. In addition to supporting the dam projects, the Forest Service wanted to approve the construction of summer homes on Jenny and Leigh lakes and allow limited logging in the region. With their ability to rubber-stamp these projects usurped, the Forest Service became bitter, developing a grudge that would continue to manifest opposition to the NPS in Jackson Hole for decades.

Finally, the protection of the scenic lakes became an omen of goodwill between the Park Service and the dude wranglers. The opposition of Struthers Burt and his ilk was not to the Park Service necessarily, but rather what was understood to be the *effects* of a national park; namely, the crowding of big-chain hotels and mobs of tourists uninterested in the rustic experience offered by the dude ranches. Albright and Burt *were* aligned in their desire to see the landscape protected from development; its rugged, wild quality was, after all, a critical asset for the dude-ranching business. Ever the savvy strategist,

Albright "let writer-dude rancher Struthers Burt and the others in the Jackson Hole group know that [he] was siding with them in fighting the dams."[33]

At the center of the conflict was the question of who Struthers Burt and company could trust. Embodying the suspicion of oversight that is characteristic of the Western rugged individualism that the Jackson Hole pioneers were inundated with, the dam debacle forced them to make a choice. Would they side with the U.S. Forest Service that represented less scrutiny but greater development? Or would they ally themselves with the National Park Service's preservation mission, despite the regulations that came with it?

"Burt and the other Jackson Hole protectors still were not ready to back addition of the area to Yellowstone National Park," wrote Horace Albright. "However, they did begin to think in terms of some sort of federal recreation area, perhaps under the jurisdiction of the National Park Service."[34]

On July 26, 1923, prominent citizens of Jackson Hole gathered to declare their position. Horace Albright was invited to a secret meeting held at the cabin of Maud Noble, a middle-aged woman who owned the nearby ferry across the Snake River. Horace Albright found Struthers Burt, newspaperman Richard Winger, rancher Jack Eynon, and general store-owner J.R. Jones. These men, representing various business interests and perspectives, presented their shared conclusion to Albright: recreation and preservation was the future of the valley. What they offered Albright was a compromise position: they opposed wrapping Jackson Hole into Yellowstone, but they were willing to welcome the National Park Service.

With the (albeit tepid) approval of the local community, Albright was encouraged to continue the park-making process by the decision of the Coordinating Commission on National Parks and Forests. Across the nation, competition for control of natural resources between the National Park Service and the U.S. Forest Service had prompted the need for a referee. President Calvin Coolidge created the CCNPF to settle a range of border disputes, including around Yellowstone and Jackson Hole. In October 1925, the Commission recommended creating a 100,000-acre national park unit in Teton country.

Legislation to create the park unit—which was intended to be a detached part of Yellowstone—was introduced in 1926. The effect of that bill would be slowly shaped by time and the need for compromise. Like those who met at Maud Noble's cabin in 1923, the residents of Jackson Hole weren't ready to hand over total control of the landscape to the federal government. Wyoming Senator John Kendrick went to great lengths to be sure that the interests of his constituents were represented as the bill took its final form. Echoing the sentiments of Struthers Burt's correspondence with Frank Mondell back in 1918, the legislation promised no new roads or hotels, protecting the established dude-ranching industry. Satisfied that he was properly representing his constituents, Kendrick escorted the bill through the chambers of Congress and to the president's desk in 1929.

The new national park site it created was very different from what Horace Albright had envisioned. The primary difference was that it was not an extension of Yellowstone—it was a brand-new Grand Teton National Park. But it also failed to take in the full territory that was considered necessary to protect the landscape, its wildlife, and its character. The boundaries encompassed only the Teton mountain range itself, plus Jenny and Leigh lakes. It was a mere 150 square miles, preserving the landscape only as a small painting would, framing in its best scenery and ignoring the expansive context that surrounded it. It did not match Horace Albright's ideal image of a national park for the Tetons—and that ideal image would drive his pursuit for something better.

The Coming of the Rockefellers

Over the course of the 1920s, as momentum grew for the "mountains and lakes only" Grand Teton National Park, the pendulum of public opinion had swung in favor of preservation. In Jackson Hole, the agricultural economic malaise that would contribute toward the coming Great Depression was already beginning to play out. High cattle prices driven by the Great War had dropped off and the inherent difficulties of ranching in the valley made themselves as obvious as ever. Like those who gathered in secret at Maud Noble's cabin in 1923, many began to accept that the future of the valley was in tourism.

Public opinion favoring the National Park Service—or at least the fluid concept of a recreation area—was solidified in a petition circulated in 1925. Around one hundred Jackson Hole landowners signed the petition. More than just signaling their support for the *idea* of a national park, they put practical force behind it, stating that they would "at any time... sell our ranches at what we consider a fair price."[35] For many, commitment wasn't a simple act of altruism; many ranchers were in financial crisis and the sale of their land to "whatever agency, state or national, is considered best" was an economic escape route.

Already, the concept that private property would need to be purchased and turned over to the federal government was percolating in the minds of park proponents. At the Maud Noble cabin meeting, a plan was formed to raise funds from rich friends in the east to purchase ranches in the northern part of Jackson Hole. Lacking the proper connections, this fundraising mission carried out by the settlers themselves was a flop. Fortunately, they'd invited a high-ranking National Park Service official into their confidence, one with greater experience networking among elites. Through Horace Albright, superintendent of Yellowstone and future NPS director, a great benefactor of Grand Teton National Park would be found.

In the midst of these events in Jackson Hole, John D. Rockefeller, Jr., heir to the Standard Oil fortune, made his first adult visit to Yellowstone National Park in 1924. Traveling incognito, he and his sons were making a tour of several western parks including Mesa Verde, Yosemite, and Glacier. Rockefeller expressly prohibited special attention or fanfare, traveling under the pseudonym "Mr. Davison." Like many visitors to national parks past and present, John D. Rockefeller, Jr., was seeking respite from the whirl of modern life. He wanted his sons to breathe fresh air, swim in clear water, and enjoy the effects of wilderness that place all of humanity, rich and poor, on the same level.

Horace Albright was given explicit instructions by NPS Director Stephen Mather to "absolutely not talk business" with the Rockefeller party. Undoubtedly Albright bit his lip throughout their visit. Rockefeller had already made significant donations of money and property to the National Park Service, contributing to the creation of Acadia National Park in Maine and a new museum in Mesa Verde National Park. In 1924, Albright was still overcoming the stinging defeat of the Yellowstone extension and lacked the clairvoyance to know that a below-standard park (in his opinion) would be created in 1929. "If he could see the possibilities presented by the majestic Tetons and the Jackson Hole area, he undoubtedly could help make my dreams come true," wrote Albright regarding Rockefeller's first visit.[36] Strategically, Albright arranged for the Rockefeller party to visit Jackson Lake, but restrained from making any other moves toward his ambitions.

In 1926, Rockefeller returned to Yellowstone. Albright was elated to receive a second opportunity: "This time there were no restrictions and I was free to talk to Rockefeller about anything I pleased, acting as his host and guide." The Yellowstone superintendent wasted no time, arranging a family automobile tour of Jackson Hole and accommodating them at the Jackson Lake Lodge. That evening they were treated to a view that could turn anyone into an ally for preservation: the romantic, pastoral presentation of the sun descending behind the Teton range, with a handful of moose grazing in the foregrou nd.[37]

The next day's scenery was not quite so spectacular. As they drove through the valley, the deteriorating remains of frontier life—now crumbling beneath financial burdens—were displayed before Rockefeller. From their open-air cars they viewed "a woebegone old dance hall, some dilapidated cabins, a burned-out gasoline station, a few big billboards, and here and there a sign advertising cattle range land for sale."

In the course of twenty-four hours, the contrast of these two images—the pristine natural beauty of Jackson Hole from the previous night against the defunct ruins of privatization and development—had exactly the effect that Horace Albright intended. "Mr. Albright, what would it cost to clear up all of this?" Rockefeller inquired as they approached Jenny Lake. Albright explained, "I have no idea—but we don't have any control over most it anyways, because it is privately owned."

John D. Rockefeller, Jr. Courtesy NPS History Collection.

"Well, send me an estimate as to what it would take to buy the land and clear the junk out of this area... and send me a map." John D. Rockefeller, Jr. had cracked the door open for Horace Albright's aspirations.

Never one to waste an opportunity, Albright approached the issue again as the Rockefeller family took in a second Teton sunset. He laid out the whole sequence of events: the defeat of the Yellowstone extension, the growth of local support, the disappointing plan for mountains-and-lakes-only Grand Teton National Park, and his desire to see the entire valley preserved. The Rockefellers took it all in, but failed to give Albright the immediate response he was hoping for. "I felt a little let down. Here I had laid out my fondest dream, and there was no word of comment. In fact, during the rest of the time we spent camping together there was no reference to the subject."

Feeling that the pitch for his grand plan had failed, Albright went about preparing the cost estimates and map that Rockefeller had requested for removing the Jackson Hole detritus. He enlisted Richard Winger, one of the members of the Maud Noble cabin meeting, to assemble the data. Winger estimated a cost of $397,000 to purchase and clear 14,000 acres on the scenic west side of the Snake River. Anxious about the high cost and Rockefeller's tepid response to his grand plan, Albright nevertheless presented the information when he next had the opportunity to visit Rockefeller in the east.

As Rockefeller looked over the maps, his disapproval was clear on his face. Horace Albright's heart sunk into his stomach.

"'No, no that is not what I had in mind at all,' he said. You took us that afternoon to a hill where we looked out over the mountains and the whole valley. The shadows were falling across the land, and you discussed an ideal project. I remember you used the word dream. *That's* the area for which I wanted you to get cost estimates. The family's only interested in an ideal project. And it would please me very much if you would get me data on that."[38]

The ideal project, as Albright would envision and gather data for, encompassed 100,000 acres on both sides of the Snake River and north of the town of Jackson. Richard Winger estimated that it would cost at least one million dollars—likely more. Around four hundred individual landowners held title to the landscape targeted for preservation. When purchases were complete, John D. Rockefeller, Jr., planned to donate it to the National Park Service, ensuring the permanent preservation of Jackson Hole.

It was a high cost and an ambitious plan. Rockefeller stamped his approval without much additional consideration. The cost and effort seemed to matter little to him—he was only interested in an ideal project.

Snake River Land Company

In the summer of 1927, agents of Rockefeller incorporated the Snake River Land Company. It was cast as a sportsman's company, interested in buying land for continued elk management. Following Horace Albright's advice, Rockefeller's association with the company—and its true purpose of purchasing land to donate to the National Park Service—was held in deep secrecy. Keeping these details locked away would make the work of the Snake River Land Company as efficient as possible. If it was known that Rockefeller was associated with the project, speculators would rush to make homestead claims and land prices would skyrocket. If Albright and the NPS were known to be involved, they risked re-awakening anti-Park Service sentiments.

To cloak the corporation in confidentiality, the Snake River Land Company (SRLC) was formed in Salt Lake City rather than New York. Vanderbilt Webb and Harold Fabian, both attorneys, were chosen to serve as president and vice president respectively. Jackson Hole banker Robert Miller was chosen to be the field agent responsible for brokering land sales. Not even Miller knew the true purpose of the SRLC, demonstrating just how tightly held the secret was. In previous years, Miller had been an aggressive opponent of Yellowstone extension and required assurances that the land he purchased wouldn't be used to increase Park Service presence in Jackson Hole. Undoubtedly he never would have signed on to the SRLC if he had known who was really behind it.

Though the veiled motives of the Snake River Land Company were altruistic, it was necessary for it to behave *as a business.* It was only aligned with the National Park Service behind closed doors; to all observers, it was a venture that needed to buy at low cost and make a profit. As a result, Robert Miller (and later Richard Winger) were encouraged to drive hard bargains. In any negotiation, it is difficult to reach a deal when there isn't a perceived winner and loser. Such was the case in Jackson Hole, though the SRLC always contended (and later analysis has supported) that land was always purchased at a fair price (around $40 per acre on average).[39]

Despite all attempts at being fair—which required taking into consideration complex variables like the condition of a property, its improvements, and location—many residents experienced regret and resentment when the true intent of the SRLC was revealed. Some residents would contend that they had sold under economic duress or as a result of illegal coercion. Hearings held in 1933 would demonstrate that all bargaining tactics were well above board—and perhaps some settlers would later remember affixing their signature to the 1925 petition committing them to sell in support of a public park.

In addition to purchasing private homesteads, the Snake River Land Company purchased businesses like the original Jackson Lake Lodge. Though Rockefeller never intended to go into the concession business, the necessity of the services provided by the lodge forced the issue. To keep the management of these concessions separate from the work of the SRLC, the attorney Harold Fabian organized the creation of what became the Teton Investment Company.

Through the efforts of its land agents, the Snake River Land Company purchased more than 35,000 acres for around 1.4 million dollars by 1929. It was a considerable accomplishment, completed with skill under secrecy. Perhaps they could have been even more successful—if it weren't for a blunder that blew the whole operation open.

Rockefeller Revealed

Despite the secret of the Snake River Land Company's cash flow being largely kept, there was still potential for homesteaders—whether speculators or sincere settlers—to make new claims in Jackson Hole. To ensure that all desired landscapes could be included in the future national park, Rockefeller's allies took steps to see a huge tract of the public domain withdrawn from entry, proactively preventing any threat of future homestead claims.

In 1927, Kenneth Chorley paid a visit to Secretary of the Interior Hubert Work. Chorley was a close associate of John D. Rockefeller, Jr., and responsible for managing many of his preservation and park projects. His visit to the Interior Department was simple and successful: he requested the preemptive withdrawal of the last remaining open public domain in Jackson Hole (more than 20,000 acres), which was ordered by President Calvin Coolidge on June 7, 1927. According to later hearings, Chorley disclosed to Secretary Work that Rockefeller and company wanted the land reserved for a national park.[40] The public was told that it was for the sake of elk preservation.

As the Snake River Land Company began making its first purchases, clever individuals drew a connection to the closing of the public domain. On April 12, 1928, reporting by the *Jackson's Hole Courier* hinted at the connection between the withdrawal and purchases made by Robert Miller in a short article titled "Utah Company Buying Jackson Hole Ranches." It states:

"On July 7 last [year] a Mr. Chorley of New York, representing a group of New Yorkers interested in game conservation, was instrumental in the withdrawing of 23,000 acres of Jackson Hole Land from homestead entry. This with earlier withdrawal covers every foot of unappropriated public lands in this valley. Hence, we are of the opinion that the men instrumental in the withdrawal of July 7 last are interested in the Snake River Land Company. However, time will tell."[41]

If the reporters had looked closer at "Mr. Chorley of New York," his connection to John D. Rockefeller, Jr. would almost certainly have been revealed. In those years, Chorely was working on behalf of Rockefeller to restore colonial Williamsburg in Virginia (another partnership with the Park Service that would become Colonial National Historical Park in 1936). If his ties to Rockefeller had been revealed, the whole scheme could have been exposed. Remarkably, it wasn't—for a few years at least.

Between 1928 and spring 1930, a series of uncomfortable encounters showed Albright and Rockefeller that the secrecy of their endeavor wasn't as airtight as they hoped. In the summer of 1929, Albright received a letter from an acquaintance implying that Rockefeller's involvement in the Snake River Land Company was known. Later that summer, the *Courier* reported, "we have learned upon good authority that the Snake River Land Company is a company of rich eastern sportsmen... the purpose of it all has been somewhat clouded by mystery, but one who should know has made a remark to the effect that the lands west of the Snake River would undoubtedly be turned to the government as an addition to the Grand Teton National Park."[42]

Rather than be exposed against their will, the leadership of the Snake River Land Company chose to take control of the narrative. In April 1930 a tell-all statement was released, illuminating the true intent and inner workings of the company. On April 10, the *Courier* broadcast to the public that the land purchased was "to be perpetually preserved as a monument to American ruggedness... at a cost of substantially over $1,000,000." The article reported the project had been in the works since 1923 and that "the persistence and determination of this project finally won the interest of John D. Rockefeller, Jr.," indicting Horace Albright, Struthers Burt, and all other members of the Maud Noble Cabin Meeting as being privy to the project.[43]

Buoyed by the creation of the original Grand Teton National Park in 1929, the pendulum of public sentiment was generally in favor of the National Park Service at the time the statement was released. With the Rockefeller-Albright plan exposed, the pendulum would begin to swing back toward ill-will. At first there would be outrage and anger—after which the pendulum would stall out entirely for more than a decade.

Backlash

The revelation of the Snake River Land Company projected visions of salvation and destruction throughout the Jackson Hole community. While some understood and supported the altruistic intent of Rockefeller, Albright, and their associates, the most prominent voices rabble-roused against them. An opposition newspaper, *The Grand Teton*, was organized to voice the dissent of the citizens. Unlike the journalistically serious *Jackson's Hole Courier*, *The Grand Teton* was little more than a tabloid bully-pulpit, "intensely local with nary an iota of natural interest" and specializing in "analogy, character distortion and half truth."[44]

Politically, the anti-park faction was led by the junior Senator from Wyoming, Robert D. Carey. Carey was the former governor of Wyoming (1919-1923) and had a complex relationship with the NPS in his state. He harbored resentment for Horace Albright (now serving as director of the NPS) that had developed during Albright's tenure in Yellowstone. Carey felt that Albright had not properly involved him in park-related issues. In regards to Grand Teton National Park, Carey was willing to voice support for it—but only behind closed doors. When placed before his constituents, he found it politically expedient to embody the anti-oversight rugged individualism common among westerners and opposed the park.

Over the course of three years, Robert Carey took several jabs at the park plans, putting his full political weight behind each swing. He declared that he would only support the Grand Teton expansion if the entire state voted for it in a special election. He also announced a plan to have Rockefeller turn over more than 30,000 acres to the state, to be managed as a state park. When these schemes were unsuccessful, Carey attempted to scare Rockefeller and the Park Service into submission with the threat of an investigation.

In all this, the Snake River Land Company and its associates remained steady in their course and confident in their methods. For his part, Horace Albright had been experiencing conflict over the matter for more than a decade, since the defeat of the first Yellowstone extension in 1919. The pro-park faction largely ignored the "vindictive, spunky, devil-may-care, master of insult" *Grand Teton* newspaper. Rockefeller Jr. mostly shrugged off Robert Carey's attempts at checkmate, holding to the vision of an "ideal project" that he and Albright had agreed upon so many years before. Like the rest of the park proponents, Rockefeller took the long view of the situation, understanding that "his thanks must come from posterity when wild life [*sic*] and primitive areas will be less abundant."[45]

Buoyed by the altruism of their objectives and a clean business record, Albright and the Snake River Land Company entered the Senate hearings with transparency. Prior to the hearings, narrative histories of the park extension plan, the Snake River Land Company, and the Teton Investment Company had been prepared and made widely available. In addition to being published in the *Jackson's Hole Courier* as letters to the editor, they were bound together and printed as a 91-page booklet titled *Mr. John D. Rockefeller, Jr.'s Proposed Gift of Land for the National Park System in Wyoming*. The exposé of a decade of advocacy and action swayed public opinion in favor of the NPS and discredited the hysterical opposition of *The Grand Teton* and Robert Carey. After three days of hearings in Jackson Hole, it was clear to the public and to the senators presiding over the matter that the dealings of Rockefeller, Albright, and the SRLC were completely above board. There was no scandal discovered on the banks of the Snake River in the summer of 1933.

Concurrent with the stones and arrows being thrown by anti-park actors, effort was still being exerted to see the Grand Teton expansion project to its end. In September 1930, a letter was sent and signed by pro-park citizens to the Senate Special Committee on Wild Life [sic] Resources. The letter's content became known as the "Jackson Hole Plan." It was a roadmap to take the "ideal project" and transform it into a real park through practical means. Core to the plan was using the acreage Rockefeller had acquired on both banks of the Snake River to expand Grand Teton National Park—and it was hoped that a government appropriation could be used to purchase additional land beyond that. Cattle would be allowed to travel through the park in limited areas and grazing would be allowed in the upper Gros Ventre region. Finally, it was proposed that Teton County should be compensated for the loss in property tax revenue that would result from 35,000 acres being turned over to the federal governme nt.[46]

Though the reaction to the Rockefeller revelation spurred the involvement of national and state-level politicians, the most important supporters of the park project were still the people of Jackson Hole. To that end, Struthers Burt took to the pages of the *Courier* in the summer of 1930, making the case for the park in plain economic terms. This letter to the editor stands in clear contrast to his 1919 opposition letter; reiterating the pattern in Jackson Hole that initial resistance was transformed into support when tangible benefits were demonstrated. In defense of the "The Snake River Company" Burt explained the positive effect that Rockefeller's money had already had on what pioneers remained and their descendants:

"Into this comparatively worthless country The Snake River Company came and up to the present has spent almost a million dollars. A million cold cash that had never been there before and never would have been there had it not been for [them]... Mortgages were cleared, frozen assets were liquidated, and the whole financial status of Jackson Hole was lifted."

While still avoiding arguments based purely on idealism and sentiment, Burt also defended the National Park Service. Referring to the economic impact of national parks throughout the nation, "any country that has one of 'Uncle Sam's picnic grounds' near at hand needn't worry about the future," he stated. "It all depends upon whether you wish to take the long view or the short view, upon whether you are penny wise or dollar wise, upon whether you are a far-sighted business man or a near-sighted one."[47]

It was the far-sightedness of John D. Rockefeller, Jr., that made the expansion of Grand Teton National Park possible. As posterity has shown, it would take even greater patience and determination than had already been displayed in order for the ideal project to be completed.

Stalled out

Despite being exonerated of misdeeds and the continued support of dude wranglers, the Jackson Hole Plan struggled to regain momentum. Support was needed from various factions, governmental and local, for the enlargement of Grand Teton National Park to be a sure-fire success. Support waxed and waned among Jackson Hole residents, the U.S. Forest Service, Wyoming politicians, and conservationists, producing only fleeting glimpses of agreement. Relatively minor issues repeatedly stalled the process, wasting whatever consensus had been achieved.

In 1934, Senator Robert Carey, who had been swayed by the hearings and local testimony to support the park, introduced an expansion bill. Defined by compromise between pure preservation and local interest, the bill essentially followed the Jackson Hole Plan espoused in the 1930 letter signed by Richard Winger. Concessions were given to the Forest Service and Bureau of Reclamation; cattle ranchers were promised a right-of-way to drive their herds between pastures. Teton County would be reimbursed for lost tax revenue and lands west of the Snake River would be handed over to the Park Service. The greatest compromise concerned the lands east of the

Snake—they would be managed by the Biological Survey (predecessor of the U.S. Fish and Wildlife Service) rather than the NPS.

Crafted to please all parties, it seemed certain that this proposal would bring the project to completion, though not in its ideal Albright-Rockefeller form. As often happens, intricate matters of bureaucracy got in the way. The federal Bureau of the Budget objected to allowing Teton County to be compensated for lost tax revenue by the federal government, citing the dangerous precedent it would create. If Washington delivered a pay-out for Grand Teton National Park, what was to stop counties across the west from requesting their own windfall when new national parks were established?

Though a second bill was introduced in 1935, its compromises ran even deeper, to the point that even the Park Service pulled its support. Undergirding this was a rift developing in conservation circles over a definition of the "standards" that national parks should meet. In 1929, Michigan Representative and NPS ally Louis C. Cramton wrote, "the great danger for Congress, because of its enthusiasm for national parks, is that we may go too far and create too many parks and some of them of a character that would lower the National Park standards. As a matter of fact the term 'National Park'... ought to indicate outstanding merit."[48] In essence, there was growing concern that "inferior landscapes" would be afforded national park status, diluting the value of the system and insulting the grandeur of Yosemite, Yellowstone, and Mt. Rainier, after which the whole park system was modeled.

This purist stance was championed by the leadership of what is now the National Parks Conservation Association (1919) and the Wilderness Society (1935).[49] Both were created to defend against encroaching development and the loss of primeval character in the national parks specifically and public lands more broadly. Robert Sterling Yard, who had been an instrumental publicist in the establishment of the National Park Service, was involved in the leadership of both. As editor of the *National Parks Bulletin*, he published arguments in defense of a high standard of scenery and wilderness being maintained in the national parks.

Yard took specific aim at the Jackson Hole plan in a February 1936 issue of the *National Parks Bulletin*. In an editorial titled "Losing our Primeval System in Vast Expansion," Yard derided the "addition of another Biological Survey Game Preserve, three irrigation reservoirs, large areas of National Forest, commercial traffic ways, grazing lands, dude ranches, and plain desert to Grand Teton National Park." From the perspective of Yard and other purists, the lands east of the Snake River were nothing more than desert and sagebrush—completely unremarkable and undeserving of park protection. Even more troubling was the proposal to include Jackson Lake, an artificial reservoir that might set precedent for future water development projects in other parks. In the same issue Yard included a full-page image of the Jackson Lake dam with the caption "IMAGINE THIS, IF YOU CAN, LEGISLATED INTO THE GRAND TETON NATIONAL PARK."[50] The inclusion of the sagebrush flats and artificial lake were precisely the sort of "inferior" landscapes that Yard and his associates feared would dilute the entire national park system.

In the greater scheme, the Jackson Hole Plan sat on the edge of a shift in the concept of what a national park should be. In the early years of the park system, preservation was focused on landscapes with monumental scenery, such as the great gorges of Yosemite, Zion, and the Grand Canyon. In 1933, a reorganization ordered by President Franklin Delano Roosevelt moved American battlefields and other historic sites under the jurisdiction of the Park Service. Additionally, landscapes like Indiana Dunes and the Everglades were being considered by the Park Service not for their *scenic* value, but for their *ecological* value. Indeed, the ecological significance of Jackson Hole for migrating elk herds was one of the original arguments for national park designation. Over the course of the coming decades, as the scientific understanding of ecology took root in the environmental movement of the 1960s, park proponents would embrace these new values as contributing to the national park "standard." In the 1940s, old-school preservationists were reacting to the beginnings of this shift, prompting them to oppose "inferior" parks and suggest the creation of a new designation of "National Primeval Parks." Grand Teton was recommended for this higher status.[51]

At a time when the National Park Service could have compromised on the issue and disavowed the lands east of the Snake, Director Arno Cammerer clung to the ideal. He maintained that the Teton Range and Jackson Hole were one landscape, inseparable from each other. For as long as Jackson Hole remained outside park boundaries, Grand Teton would be incomplete. Expanded more broadly, the protection of Jackson Hole was understood to be the completion of Yellowstone National Park. It was, after all, the passage of elk herds between the two landscapes that had sparked intrigue in a national park back in 1882. "This unit should have been created in 1872, but it was not. Now the opportunity was manifest to *restore* and preserve this biotic unit."[52]

To this end, the late 1930s saw another attempt to swing the pendulum of public opinion back toward the National Park Service. It was soundly rebuffed when the anti-park faction called new hearings in 1938, temporarily affording them the upper hand. As a result, the conservation conflict around Jackson Hole and the Tetons would stretch into its third decade. Though he had resigned from the Park Service in 1933 to take a job as president of a mining company, Horace Albright remained heavily involved in the park effort. "It was discouraging to see so many years pass and so many of the minor skirmishes fought and won without apparent progress towards achieving the Grand Teton Park enlargement," he wrote.[53]

In all of this, there was a single individual who maintained simple, practical control over the matter: John D. Rockefeller, Jr. Over the course of the 1930s, as public opinion flip-flopped, legislation failed, and preservationists squabbled over matters of philosophy, he fixated on the vision of an ideal project. For more than a decade in some cases, Rockefeller maintained the acres purchased by the Snake River Land Company. Property taxes in the tens of thousands of dollars were paid and great expense was taken to remove dilapidated structures in an attempt to restore the rustic western character to the landscape. Despite his resolve, Rockefeller would grow discouraged after a decade of uncertainty and great personal expense far beyond the original estimates. In 1942, he would issue an ultimatum.

National Monument

In March 1943, Olaus Murie, an elk biologist and leader in The Wilderness Society, drove into the town of Jackson after recording winter elk fatalities. He and his wife, Mardie, lived in Jackson Hole on assignment with the Biological Survey. He noticed a crowd on the sidewalk, incensed over some piece of news. "Haven't you heard what they've done? The President has put our whole valley in a park!"[54]

After more than two decades, the dream of John D. Rockefeller and Horace Albright came true. It didn't happen through a legislative process with all necessary parties in agreement; that had been tried and deemed impossible. Rather, President Franklin D. Roosevelt signed an executive order combining the Rockefeller lands with tracts of the Teton National Forest and other holdings to create Jackson Hole National Monument. Roosevelt received this power from the 1906 Antiquities Act, a powerful conservation tool that could place a protective shield over federal landscapes by presidential proclamation. The Antiquities Act was written in response to the vandalism and looting of southwestern archeological sites like Mesa Verde and Chaco Canyon. As such, the law required that landscapes could only be preserved if they harbored historic or scientific resources of national importance.

Throughout the course of the early 20th century, the designation of national monuments was seen as an efficient—and often emergency—tool for landscape preservation. The first national monument, Devil's Tower, was proclaimed by Theodore Roosevelt in 1906. Among many landscapes and archeological sites, Roosevelt proclaimed monuments for Arizona's Petrified Forest and Washington's Olympic range. Both monuments were created specifically to halt destructive mining and logging, respectively. Both Olympic and Petrified Forest were later transformed into national parks by Congress. With all national monuments in 1943 under NPS jurisdiction, the creation of Jackson Hole National Monument effectively completed the "ideal project." It was a de facto expansion of Grand Teton National Park—they were separate units in name, but together form one intact landscape.

After years of indecision and impasse, the creation of Jackson Hole National Monument was swift and certain. It came to be as a culminating act of resolve by John D. Rockefeller, Jr. In November 1942, he wrote to Interior Secretary Harold Ickes, stating that if the government didn't intend to accept the land, he would move to sell it within the year. His patience had grown thin and the funds he was willing to commit had dried up. It was time for another entity—National Park Service or otherwise—to take over responsibility for the lands acquired by the Snake River Land Company.[55]

This letter triggered actions that had already been considered within the Interior Department. As history has shown, the use of the Antiquities Act can be controversial, provoking accusations of dictatorship and dispossession. Despite the fickleness of public opinion in Jackson Hole, the NPS was serious enough about using the Antiquities Act to write a draft proclamation in 1939. In 1940, acting NPS director Arthur Demaray wrote to Secretary Ickes with the opinion that "the establishment of the area as a national monument at the appropriate time appears to be the only course available."[56]

Now, with an impasse in Congress and an ultimatum issued by Rockefeller—take the land or see it sold—the time had come. In full support, Secretary Ickes took control of the matter and brought it before President Roosevelt. FDR was no stranger to exercising the power of the Antiquities Act, proclaiming twenty monuments over the course of his four terms. Ickes warned Roosevelt that this monument was likely to be extremely controversial. Undeterred, the president affixed his signature to the proclamation on March 15, 1943.

As Ickes had predicted, public sentiment was immediately hostile. Olaus Murie wrote, "Signs appeared in the windows of many business houses: 'We are opposed to Jackson Hole National Monument.'"[57] Local opposition had a voice in the new editor of the Jackson Hole *Courier*, Charles Kratzer. On March 22, 1943, he published a special edition of the *Courier* with the sole purpose of condemning the monument. Front page headlines trumpeted the intent of Wyoming's congressmen to have it abolished. An editorial predicted "it now looks quite probable that Jackson Hole will soon be able to enjoy the distinction of having been the shortest-lived national monument on record."[58]

Despite decades of messaging by the Park Service, misinformation around government overreach and the local economy was weaponized by the anti-park faction. Rumors circulated that ranchers were being kicked off their land and that the county would soon be destitute from the loss of tax revenue. The opposition harnessed the rhetoric of the ongoing Second World War, calling

Roosevelt's proclamation "a foul, sneaking Pearl Harbor Move," and likened it to the Nazi annexation of Austria.[59]

At a time when news from the front lines in Europe and Asia should have dominated the headlines, the alleged authoritarianism in Jackson Hole managed to break through into the national consciousness. Two months after the presidential proclamation, a group of heavily armed ranchers drove more than 500 cattle across the monument. They were led by film celebrity Wallace Beery, whose stardom captured the attention of the national media. *Time* circulated the story first, later to be syndicated through the gamut of news publications. Understanding that the cattle drive was a stunt intended to grab attention and spark a conflict, Park Service officials ignored it. The trespass demonstrated just how provocative the anti-park propaganda was; park proponents had, after all, included concessions for exactly this sort of cattle drive in previous attempts at expansion, showing their awareness and sympathy for the issue.

Immediate local opposition was also manifest in the Teton National Forest, specifically at the ranger stations included in the transfer of 130,000 acres to the Park Service. The local hires who staffed these outposts were instructed to vacate the premise, along with Forest Service equipment and property. In an expression of their bitterness towards the Park Service, the Forest Service staff interpreted these instructions liberally. The Jackson Lake Ranger Station was left completely uninhabitable;

cabinets and cupboards stripped, plumbing gutted, doors removed, floor joists severed, a water tank exhumed from the ground. The Kelly Ranger Station faced a similar fate. Later that summer, a vandal trapped a live skunk in the Jackson Lake Station, which promptly died.[60]

As local opposition took the form of crimes and misdemeanors, Wyoming politicians sought legal means to abolish Jackson Hole National Monument. In 1943, Congressman Frank Barrett introduced legislation to undo the monument, which quickly moved through both the House and the Senate. Proud of his expansive conservation record, there was no realistic chance that Roosevelt would rescind his own proclamation by signing the bill. He exercised a pocket veto, letting the bill die on his desk as the Congressional term timed out.

Of course, at the core of the issue was whether or not the President was justified in his creation of a park by fiat. This topic was taken up by the State of Wyoming, which sued to have the executive order overturned. In *State of Wyoming v. Franke* (named for the superintendent of Grand Teton National Park), the state asserted that its rights were being trespassed on and that it stood to suffer financial harm. More significantly, it argued that the president had misused the Antiquities Act to create Jackson Hole National Monument. The suit claimed that the proclamation was "outside the scope and purpose of the Antiquities Act under which the Proclamation was issued in that such area contains no objects of an [*sic*] historic or scientific interest required by the Act."[61] To defend this crucial component of Roosevelt's legal use of the 1906 act, evidence was mustered to prove that Jackson Hole did indeed harbor historic and scientific interest. Entered into evidence was the presence of fur trappers like John Colter in the area and the ecological importance of the valley to the elk herds.

In the end, Judge T. Blake Kennedy didn't rule on whether the historic and scientific qualities of Jackson Hole met muster. The case was dismissed, the judge ruling that "in short, this seems to be a controversy between the Legislative and Executive Branches of the Government in which, under the evidence presented here, the Court cannot interfere." If Wyoming wanted justice for the perceived slight of a new national park unit, it would have to pursue the matter in the halls of Congress.

To that end, Representative Frank Barrett would continue to introduce legislation to repeal Jackson Hole National Monument. Each time, the bill never made it to a vote on the House floor. As the foul prophecies of economic ruin and homeless ranchers failed to come true, anti-park momentum dissolved. Within just a few years, Jackson Hole National Monument would be abolished—to be replaced with a new Grand Teton National Park.

The Ideal Accomplished

On December 16, 1949, a ceremony was held in which John D. Rockefeller, Jr. officially deeded title to 33,562 acres of land to the federal government. With the monument's future uncertain, Rockefeller had deemed it safest to maintain control of land he'd purchased. Now, with the winds of change breezing across the sagebrush, Rockefeller believed the time had come.

By late 1949, all legal attempts to undo Jackson Hole National Monument had failed. Post-war tourism was booming in the valley, bringing the economic benefits long promised by the Park Service. Public opinion was swinging back toward favor. Debate continued over the worthiness of Jackson Hole as part of a national park, but conservationists were able to place the ideals of the project over their individual opinions on the matter. Only a small coalition of local businessmen and ranchers continued to oppose Park Service-style preservation. Politicians who had at times fiercely opposed the project gathered to find a permanent solution.

The issues that remained to be resolved were the same as before—anxiety over grazing rights, management of the elk, and the loss of taxes for Teton County. The concerned parties were consulted and agreements were reached. Ranchers and their direct heirs would maintain their grazing leases. Responsibility for the elk would be shared by the state of Wyoming and the federal government. It was allowed that if the population grew too large, the Park Service would temporarily deputize local hunters as rangers to reduce the herds. Though the Bureau of the Budget still objected, a plan was hammered out to reimburse the county for lost revenue.

Perhaps the most consequential compromise was a provision inserted at the start of the bill that "no further extension or establishment of national parks or monuments in Wyoming may be undertaken except by express authorization of the Congress." This stipulation effectively banned future uses of the Antiquities Act in the state. With the consent of all necessary parties, the bill sailed through Congress. It was signed by President Harry Truman on September 14, 1950. The ideal Grand Teton National Park had been created.

Reminiscing on the victory, Horace Albright wrote that "it had been twenty-five years since that summer day in 1926 when I had shown the Rockefeller family the Jackson Hole lands that needed to be added to the national park system." Seventy-six years old when the bill passed, Rockefeller wrote to his friend and ally that it "must have brought you hardly less satisfaction than it brought me. What a pleasure it has been to work with you in this matter over the years."[62]

Over the course of those decades, Albright, Rockefeller, their agents and allies had encountered numerous obstacles on the path to preservation. Each was an opportunity to settle. They might have been satisfied with the 1929 "mountains and lakes" park or retreated when the Snake River Land Company was exposed. The risks of a national monument controversy could have been deemed too great. They could have caved to the criticisms of the preservation purists. The project could have stalled until Rockefeller eventually divested out of frustration. Despite these opportunities for something less than the ideal, their vision for a national park in the Teton country prevailed.

In doing so, they carried forth a vision for the landscapes that stretched back to Struthers Burt's decision to stay in the valley in 1908 and the explorers who had come before him. The future of this land—the thrust of the Teton range, the twisting of the Snake River, and the view of it all across Jackson Hole—was now in humankind's forever reserved ability to experience it.

POSTSCRIPT

M ARCH 14, 2026.

As I write this, America has witnessed an unprecedented erosion of what is often called our "Best Idea." Across the last 150 years, America's public lands have had their share of dark days; parks left in protection-less limbo before the establishment of the NPS, the lean budgets during and after WWII, and the lopsidedly pro-extraction tenure of Interior Secretary James G. Watt, to name a few. Today, our national parks face all those threats at once, accelerated and exacerbated by administrators who see public lands as nothing more than assets on a balance sheet.[1] Staff have been recklessly fired or coerced into early retirement; Baseline appropriations for public operations are being used as political bargaining chips; Wilderness areas and sacred landscapes are being targeted for energy development projects; It is a torrent of attacks, undercutting the nation's public land legacy and tilting it towards collapse.

Despite the dark days in which I have written and revised this book, I've found a small comfort in taking the long view. As Americans, our interaction with the natural world and the value we placed on wilderness has ebbed and flowed over the past 150 years. The public lands system we enjoy today—of which our national parks are the core—wouldn't exist if we did not continually return to the inherent good of preservation. It is a virtuous network of roadless lands, scenic highways, wildlife migration corridors, monuments to human heroism and tragedy, visitor centers and backcountry sites, endangered species habitats and picnic grounds, all established because enough people agreed across the decades *that they should be.*

During times when our public land "stewards" prioritize extraction above all else, we must remember that Yellowstone National Park was born because natural wonders were being misused. Whether for scamming tourists or stripping out timber, 19th century economics were not considerate towards the nation's scenic and natural resources. It was the rapid disappearance of wild animals—from egrets in the Everglades to elk in Jackson Hole—that prompted the creation of wildlife refuges and civil societies for their preservation. It was the impending Tragedy of the Commons resulting from runaway logging and mining that created the need for our national forest system. It was the risk of scenic wonders being monopolized and privatized that made the establishment of Yellowstone National Park urgent. Out of dire circumstances came one of America's greatest and most virtuous cultural achievements. In both the story of Yellowstone and the national park system it initiated, you find a clear expression of democratic values: that a heritage and a place would be preserved by a generation not for their own benefit, but for the benefit of their descendants stretching into perpetuity.

Of course, the hymns of praise to the national park idea and its democratic core ring tragically hollow for many. The chorus dies out quickly when we consider the people who benefitted from landscape preservation—and who they intended to preserve it from. As has been thoroughly demonstrated throughout this book, the wealthy, elite conservationists saw the end users of the national parks as being similar to themselves. In that vision, exclusion—whether intentional or not—was part of the project. The broad democratic core of land preservation, one that includes communities of life stretching to non-human species and unborn generations, fundamentally excluded certain groups from the outset.

In the stories included here, this is most apparent in Glacier National Park and the dispossession of the Blackfeet. Like the deep hues of alpenglow painting the mountains blood-red, understanding the cruelty enacted against the Blackfeet Nation should re-color how we perceive the land. The tragedy cannot be undone or ignored; it is part of the landscape. If you allow the land to speak to you, you must afford it the opportunity to tell this story of inhumanity. You must allow it to do the most important work of history, pricking you such that it draws the blood of those whose land was stolen and allows you to feel what small part of their experience is possible. The swelling of empathy should motivate us to engage the work of restoration. The pain of the past is not a prompt to declare Glacier Park impure and cast it aside; it is an opportunity to join with those that understand the past so as to work towards justice for the Blackfeet.

For me, joining that effort meant centering the history told here of Glacier National Park's origin on the Blackfeet. In the grand scheme of things, it is the passive role of the storyteller—but it is the role I'm equipped to perform. Others are equipped to engage the work of restoration more practically, particularly those who live in and know that land.

In 2023, in partnership with the National Park Service, the Blackfeet Nation released a small herd of bison into Glacier National Park. The reintroduction of bison to Glacier—from which they were eradicated as part of the 19th century strategy of Indigenous cultural destruction—represents a step towards restoration. After releasing the bison, Blackfeet leaders released a statement saying:

"Today we are expressing our sovereignty, claiming our reserved rights, reversing this ecological deterioration, overturning this incalculable cultural loss, writing historic wrongs, and preparing a powerful path for a successful future — the path of Iinniiwa [bison]."[2]

Grazing beneath Chief Mountain, the reintroduction of the bison can't be expected to undo all the injustices of the past. In many ways, it is just a symbol—but so are the national parks, and they have not failed to inspire noble and generous actions across the generations.

Even as we see positive developments in some corners of our national park system, we must vigilantly defend against old attacks. Echoes of the strong sentiments expressed after the creation of Jackson Hole National Monument reverberates in the American West today, especially in the state of Wyoming. In early 2025, a committee in the Wyoming state legislature supported a measure asking Congress to turn over all federal lands in the state except Yellowstone. This came after Wyoming joined a failed lawsuit launched by the state of Utah seeking to wrest away millions of acres from federal control. In Wyoming, it included Grand Teton National Park.[3] These are just a few in a slew of efforts over the last decades to weaken the Antiquities Act. Over the years, multiple bills have been introduced to repeal the act or reduce its power, written to require the President to get prior approval from Congress to declare a national monument—the same provision included in the law creating Grand Teton National Park.

As we face these attacks on America's rich tradition of landscape preservation, we should continue to let history be our guide. There will always be threats to our shared landscapes and the laws that preserve them—but none of them are new. They are the same forces that threatened Yellowstone in 1872: mindsets that see the green of forests only as the green of bank notes, philosophies that believe the land is something to be exploited rather than shared.

What will be new is how we respond to them. These landscapes will only be protected for as long as we want them to be. Do not let the stories in this book be consumed and forgotten. Take them in and join the long tradition of protecting these American lands, for all nations, generations, and communities of life.

Notes

Yellowstone National Park

1. An Act to set apart a certain Tract of Land lying near the Head-waters of the Yellowstone River as a public Park, March 1, 1872.

2. Douglas MacDonald, *Before Yellowstone: Native American Archeology in the National Park*, (Seattle: University of Washington Press, 2018) 4.

3. MacDonald, *Before Yellowstone* 68.

4. MacDonald, *Before Yellowstone*, 81.

5. MacDonald, *Before Yellowstone*, 84.

6. Sarah Hinkelman, "Hopewell Culture Obsidian," National Park Service, accessed December 16, 2025. https://www.nps.gov/articles/000/hopewell-culture-obsidian.htm

7. U.S. Department of the Interior, *Report Upon the Yellowstone National Park, to the Secretary of the Interior, by P.W. Norris, Superintendent, For the Year, 1879*. Philetus Norris. Washington, D.C., 1879. PDF. https://www.mtmemory.org/nodes/view/104719 (Accessed May 10, 2025)

8. Peter Nabokov and Laurence Loendorf, *American Indians and Yellowstone National Park: A Documentary Overview*. (United States: Yellowstone Center for Resources), retrieved from https://www.google.com/books/edition/American_Indians_and_Yellowstone_Nationa/_kr_fK5IIQkC?hl=en&gbpv=1, 102.

9. Weldon Heald, "The Yellowstone Story: Genesis of the National Park Idea," *Utah Historical Quarterly*, Vol. 28, No. 2 (1960), https://issuu.com/utah10/docs/uhq_volume28_1960_number2/s/98927

10. Horace Albright and Frank Taylor, *Oh, Ranger! A Book about the National Parks*. (California: Stanford University Press), retrieved from https://archive.org/details/ohrangerbookabou0000hora .

11. Accounts of this series of events can be found in MacDonald, *Before Yellowstone*, 29-30; Mark Spence, *Dispossessing the Wilderness: Indian Removal and the Making of the National Parks*, (Oxford: Oxford University Press, 2000), 57; Jerome Green, *Nez Perce Summer: The U.S. Army and the Nee-Me-Poo Crisis* (Montana Historical Society Press, 2000) retrieved from https://npshistory.com/publications/nepe/greene/chap8.htm .

12. Mark Spence, *Dispossessing the Wilderness: Indian Removal and the Making of the National Parks*, (Oxford: Oxford University Press, 2000), 57.

13. U.S. Department of the Interior, *Report Upon the Yellowstone National Park, to the Secretary of the Interior, by P.W. Norris, Superintendent, For the Year, 1877*. Philetus Norris. Washington, D.C., 1877. PDF. https://www.mtmemory.org/nodes/view/104717 (Accessed May 10, 2025)

14. U.S. Department of the Interior. *Annual Report of the Yellowstone National Park to the Secretary of the Interior for the Year 1880*. Philetus Norris. Washington, D.C., 1880. PDF. https://www.mtmemory.org/nodes/view/104720 (Accessed May 10, 2025)

15. Burton Harris, *John Colter: His Years in the Rockies*, (Lincoln: University of Nebraska Press, 1993),15.

16. Harris, *John Colter*, 76.

17. Truman Everts, "Thirty-Seven Days of Peril," *Scribner's Monthly*, November, 1871, https://www.gutenberg.org/files/30924/30924-h/30924-h.htm

18. Everts, "Thirty Seven Days of Peril."

19. Nathaniel Langford, *The Discovery of Yellowstone Park*, (Lincoln: University of Nebraska Press, 1972), 107.

20. Langford, *Discovery of Yellowstone*, 108.

21. "Yellowstone Papers: Full Details of the Entire Trip, Description of the Yellowstone Falls, The Mud Volcano, the Lake, the Hot Springs, The Greater Geysers in the World, etc., etc., etc.," *Weekly Rocky Mountain Gazette*, October 24, 1870; Aubrey Haines, *Yellowstone National Park: It's Exploration and Establishment* (Washington, D.C.: National Park Service, 1974).

22. Lecture by Nathaniel P. Langford, original in the manuscript collection of the Yellowstone Park Reference Library, 183, 185. Quoted in Aubrey Haines, *Yellowstone National Park: It's Exploration and Establishment* (Washington, D.C.: National Park Service, 1974), 95.

23. Jay Cooke letter to Ferdinand Vanderveer Hayden. A.B. Nettleton to Hayden, June 7, 1871. NA Microfilm 623, reel 2, frame 0120. Quoted in Haines, *Yellowstone National Park*, 95.

24. Ibid., Letter of Oct. 27, 1871. RG-57, Hayden Survey, General Letters Received, 1864, 1866-74, vol. III. Qouted in Alfred Runte, *National Parks: The American Experience*, (Essex: Lyons Press, 2021), 38; Haines, *Yellowstone National Park*, 109.

25. Langford, *Discovery of Yellowstone*, 117.

26. Ibid., 117-118.

27. Ibid., 18.

28. Henry Dawes, as recorded in *The Congressional* Globe, 42d Cong., 2d sess., pp. 1243—44, "Public Park on the Yellowstone River." Quoted in Haines, *Discovery of Yellowstone*, 123.

29. In 1916, the law that established the National Park Service built on this idea with what has become known as the "dual mandate." It states that the "purpose is to conserve the scenery and the natural and historic objects and the wild life therein and to provide for the enjoyment of the same in such manner and by such means as will leave them unimpaired for the enjoyment of future generations." This dual mandate, requiring the balance of both conservation and recreation, which are often at odds with one another, has caused confusion and controversy throughout the history of the national parks.

Glacier National Park

1. Christopher Ashby, "Blackfeet Agreement of 1895 and Glacier National Park: A Case History" *Graduate Student Theses, Dissertations, & Professional Papers* (1985), 14, https://scholarworks.umt.edu/etd/1684/

2. Treaty with the Blackfeet, Articles 9-10, October 17, 1855.

3. John Taliaferro, *Grinnell: America's Environmental Pioneer and His Restless Drive to Save the West* (New York: Liveright Publishing, 2019), 174.

4. Michael Turek and Robert Keller, *American Indians and National Parks*, (Phoenix: University of Arizona Press, 1999) 44-45.

5. Hugh Grinnell ed., *The Father of Glacier National Park: Discoveries and Explorations in His Own Words*, (Charleston, SC: The History Press, 2020), 139., 13-42

6. Taliaferro, *Grinnell*, 190.

7. George Bird Grinnell, "A Standing Menace," *Field and Stream*, December 8, 1882, quoted in Taliaferro, *Grinnell*, 203.

8. Emerson Hough and Scott Herring, ed., *Rough Trip Through Yellowstone* (Helena: Riverbend Publishing, 2013),

9. Hough, *Rough Trip*, 30.

10. Ibid., 32.

11. Taliaferro, *Grinnell*, 205.

12. Gerald A. Diettert, "Grinnell's Glacier" (1990), *Graduate Student Theses, Dissertations, & Professionally Papers*, 104.

13. Ibid., 104-105.

14. Keller and Turek, *American Indians and National Parks*, 46; Taliaferro, *Grinnell*, 219.

15. Spence, *Dispossessing the Wilderness*, 74.

16. Ashby, "A Case History, 26.

17. Diettert, "Grinnells Glacier," 106. Ibid., 104; Keller and Turek, *American Indians and National Parks*, 49; George Bird Grinnell diary, quoted in Hugh Grinnell ed., *The Father of Glacier National Park: Discoveries and Explorations in His Own Words*, (Charleston, SC: The History Press, 2020), 139.

18. Ibid., 104; Keller and Turek, *American Indians and National Parks*, 49; George Bird Grinnell diary, quoted in Hugh Grinnell ed., *The Father of Glacier National Park: Discoveries and Explorations in His Own Words*, (Charleston, SC: The History Press, 2020), 139.

19. George Bird Grinnell to Hoke Smith, July 11, 1895, quoted in *The Father of Glacier National Park*, 138.

20. Keller and Tureky, *American Indians and National Parks*, 47.

21. George Bird Grinnell, quoted in Taliaferro, *Grinnell*, 223.

22. George Bird Grinnell to George Gould, September 17, 1891, quoted in Taliaferro, *Grinnell*, 195; Diettert, "Grinnell's Glacier," 84

23. George Bird Grinnell to R.W. Gilder, Century Co., May 12, 1892, quoted in Diettert, "Grinnell's Glacier," 87.

24. George Bird Grinnell to F.J. Whitney, October 17, 1894, quoted in Taliaferro, *Grinnell*, 213-214.

25. George Bird Grinnell to F.J. Whitney, October 17, 1894., quoted in Diettert, "Grinnell's Glacier", 96.

26. Spence, *Dispossessing the Wilderness*, 79; Keller and Turek, *American Indians and National Parks*, 49

27. George Bird Grinnell, "The Crown of the Continent," *The Century Magazine*, September, 1901, https://babel.hathitrust.org/cgi/pt?id=uc1.321 06019606281&seq=657&q1=crown+of+the+continent&start=1

28. Taliaferro, *Grinnell*, 366.

29. For a detailed look at the economic benefits perceived by railroads in the creation of new national parks, Marquerite Shaffer, *See America First: Tourism and National Identity, 1880-1940,* (Washington, DC: Smithsonian Books, 2001).

30. Andrew C. Harper, "Conceiving Nature: The Creation of Montana's Glacier National Park" *Montana The Magazine of Western History,* Vol. 60, No. 2, Summer (2010), 15, https://www.jstor.org/stable/25701734

31. Harper, "Conceiving Nature", 16.

32. Joseph Dixon, *Congressional Record,* (April 14, 1910), 4832, quoted in Harper, "Conceiving Nature", 22.

33. Thomas Carter, *Congressional Record,* (January 25, 1910), 970-71, quoted in Harper, "Conceiving Nature", 18.

34. Turek and Keller, *American Indians,* 45-50.

35. Spence, *Dispossessing the Wilderness,* 81.

36. Agreement with the Blackfeet, 1895.

37. Isaac Kantor, "Ethnic Cleansing and America's Creation of National Parks" *Public Land and Resource Law Review,* Vol 28, (June 2007) 52.

38. Horace Albright, *The Birth of the National Park Service: The Founding Years,* (Salt Lake City: Howe Brothers, 1985), 276.

Grand Teton National Park

1. Struthers Burt, *Diary of a Dude Wrangler,* (Jackson: Satrugi Press, 2019), 23.

2. Wallace Stegner, *Beyond the Hundredth Meridian: John Wesley Powell and the Second Opening of the West,* (New York: Penguin, 1992).

3. Burt, *Diary,* 40.

4. Burt, *Diary,* 33.

5. Merrill Mattes, *Colter's Hell and Jackson's Hole*, (Wyoming: Yellowstone Library and Museum Association, 1980). https://www.gutenberg.org/files/50381/50381-h/50381-h.htm (accessed November 12, 2025).

6. Mattes, *Colter's Hell and Jackson's Hole* https://www.gutenberg.org/files/50381/50381-h/50381-h.htm (accessed November 12, 2025).

7. U.S. Department of War, *Report on the Exploration of the Yellowstone River. Bvt. Brig. Gen. William F. Raynolds*, William Raynolds, Washington, D.C: GPO, 1868.

8. U.S. Department of War, *Report on the Exploration of the Yellowstone River. Bvt. Brig. Gen. William F. Raynolds*.

9. William Henry Jackson, *Time Exposure: The Autobiography of William Henry Jackson*, (New York: G.P Putnam's Sons, 1940) 205.

10. U.S. Geological and Geographical Survey of the Territories, *Sixth Annual Report of the United States Geological Survey of the Territories, embracing portions of Montana, Idaho, Wyoming, and Utah, being a report of progress of the explorations of the year 1872*, Ferdinand Hayden. Washington, D.C: GPO, 1873. https://pubs.usgs.gov/publication/70038930 (accessed June 10, 2025).

11. U.S. Geological and Geographical Survey of the Territories, *Sixth Annual Report of the United States Geological Survey of the Territories, embracing portions of Montana, Idaho, Wyoming, and Utah, being a report of progress of the explorations of the year 1872*.

12. Mattes, *Colter's Hell*, John Colter, the Phantom Explorer—1807-1808.

13. U.S. Department of War, *Report on the Exploration of the Yellowstone River. Bvt. Brig. Gen. William F. Raynolds*.

14. Jackson, *Time Exposure*, Mountain of the Holy Cross.

15. John Daugherty, *A Place Called Jackson Hole: A Historic Resource Study of Grand Teton National Park*, (Moose, Wyoming: Grand Teton Natural History Association, 1999). https://www.nps.gov/parkhistory/online_books/grte2/hrst.htm (accessed June, 2025).

16. Treaty with the Eastern Shoshoni and Bannock, July 3, 1868, between the United States Government, Shoshone, and Bannock. https://treaties.okstate.edu/treaties/treaty-with-the-eastern-band-shoshoni-and-bannock-1868-1020

17. John Clayton, "Who Gets to Hunt Wyoming's Elk? Tribal Hunting Rights, U.S Law and the Bannock 'War' of 1895." *Wyohistory.org*, September 29, 2020, https://www.wyohistory.org/encyclopedia/who-gets-hunt-wyomings-elk-tribal-hunting-rights-us-law-and-bannock-war-1895

18. "The Indian War," *Chicago Tribune*, August 6, 1895, https://www.newspapers.com/article/chicago-tribune/184341868/

19. "The Bannock War," *Rome Daily Sentinel*, July 25, 1895, https://www.newspapers.com/article/daily-sentinel/184341793/

20. Ward v. Race Horse, 163 U.S. 504 (1896)

21. Robert Righter, *Crucible for Conservation: The Struggle for Grand Teton National Park*, (Moose, Wyoming: Grand Teton Nationla Park Association), 20.

22. "Obnoxious Laws," *The Billings Gazette*, July 15, 1902, https://www.newspapers.com/article/the-billings-gazette-obnoxious-laws-re/166774986/

23. Daugherty, *A Place Called Jackson Hole*, Conservationists.

24. Righter, *Crucible for Conservation*, 22-23.

25. Bureau of Biological Survey, *The Present Plight of the Jackson Hole Elk*, H.P. Sheldon, Olaus Murie, W.E. Crouch, Washington, D.C. https://npshistory.com/publications/grte/bs-12.pdf (accessed July, 2025).

26. Horace Albright, *The Birth of the National Park Service: The Founding Years*, (Salt Lake City: Howe Brothers, 1985), 40.

27. Albright, *Birth of the National Park Service*, 40.

28. Ibid., 72

29. Ibid., 99.

30. "Congressman Mondell Writes Jackson Hole Rancher Favoring Park Extension," *Jackson's Hole Courier*, October 9, 1919.

31. In the early 1900s, one of the great conservation battles fought by John Muir and the Sierra Club was to prevent the flooding of the Hetch Hetchy Valley in Yosemite National Park. Hetch Hetchy was considered by Muir and others to be just as beautiful as Yosemite. It was ultimately flooded in order to ensure a stable water supply for San Francisco. In the second half of the 20th century, battles between preservationists and water reclamation projects continued to take place and often garnered significant attention from the public. In 1950, writer Bernard DeVoto published the article "Shall we let them ruin our national parks?" which outlined the many ways that water storage projects threatened landscapes that were supposed to be preserved for future generations.

32. Righter, *Crucible for Conservation*, 32

33. Albright, *Birth of the National Park Service*, 117.

34. Ibid., 118.

35. "Hearings on S. Res. 226," 1933, pp. 266-268, in Daugherty, *A Place Called Jackson Hole*, Conservationists.

36. Albright, *Birth of the National Park Service*, 160.

37. Ibid., 163.

38. Ibid., 164-165.

39. Righter, *Crucible for Conservation*, 50-65.

40. "Hearings on S. Res. 226," 1933, pp. 76-79, in Daugherty, *A Place Called Jackson Hole*, Conservationists.

41. "Utah Company Buying Jackson Hole Ranches," *Jackson's Hole Courier*, April 12, 1928, https://www.newspapers.com/article/jacksons-hole-co urier-chorley-discovere/176423531/

42. "Ye Editor Speculates On Results of Snake River Land Company Activities," *Jackson's Hole Courier*, August 15, 1929, https://www.newspapers.com/article/jacksons-hole-courier-august-1929-specu/176424858/

43. "Snake River Land Company Officials Break Secrecy," *Jackson's Hole Courier*, April 10, 1930.

44. Righter, *Crucible for Conservation*, 71-72.

45. Ibid., 75.

46. Ibid., 69.

47. "Struthers Burt Writes of Snake River Land Company," *Jackson's Hole Courier*, June 5, 1930.

48. "A Case for National Park Standards," *Saturday Evening Post*, October 12, 1929.

49. At the time, it was called the National Parks Association. For the ease of the reader, I've chosen to use its present name.

50. Robert Sterling Yard, "Losing our Primeval System in Vast Expansion," *National Parks Bulletin*, February, 1936, https://babel.hathitrust.org/cgi/pt?id=mdp.39015001273435&seq=307

51. William Wharton, "Preservation Requires Classification," *National Parks Bulletin*, Vol. 15, No. 68, July 1940, https://npshistory.com/npca/bulletin/jul-1940.pdf (accessed July, 2025)

52. Righter, *Crucible for Conservation*, 91.

53. Albright, *Birth of the National Park Service*, 321.

54. Olaus Murie and Margaret Murie, *Wapiti Wilderness*, (Boulder: Colorado University Press, 1985),122.

55. Ibid., 322.

56. Memorandum from Arthur E. Demaray to Harold Ickes, August 1, 1940, quoted in Righter, *Crucible for Conservation*, 106; Albright, *Birth of the National Park Service*, 322.

57. Murie, *Wapiti Wilderness*,122.

58. "Citizens Meeting Sees Hope Monument Proclamation to be Declared Invalid; Protest Committee Formed," *Jackson's Hole Courier (Extra)*, March 22, 1943, https://www.newspapers.com/article/jacksons-hole-courier-special-in-the-co/176726389/

59. *Jackson Hole Courier*, May 6, 1943, quoted in Righter, *Crucible for Conservation*, 110; Ibid., 115.

60. Daughtery, A *Place Called Jackson Hole*, Conservationists.

61. *State of Wyoming v. Franke*, 58 F. Supp. 890 (D. Wyo. 1945), https://law.justia.com/cases/federal/district-courts/FSupp/58/890/1876289/

62. Albright, *Birth of the National Park Service*, 324.

Postscript: Preservation in the Present

1. Andrew Weiss, "Doug Burgum Says Public Lands are America's Balance Sheet—He's Right but for the Wrong Reasons," Center for Western Priorities, April 1, 2025, https://westernpriorities.org/2025/04/doug-burgum-says-public-lands-are-americas-balance-sheet-hes-right-but-for-the-wrong-reasons/#:~:text=America's%20public%20lands%20are%2C%20of,value%20of%20lands%20and%20nature .

2. Michael Jamison, "How We Heal," National Parks Conservation Association, 2023, https://www.npca.org/articles/3579-how-we-heal

3. Kurt Repanshek, "Wyoming Seeking Federal Land Grab, Utah Wants to Co-Manage National Parks," The National Parks Traveler, February 2, 2025. https://www.nationalparkstraveler.org/2025/02/wyoming-seeking-federal-land-grab-utah-wants-co-manage-national-parks

Bibliography

In order to reduce printing costs and provide easier access to the many online resources that were used to produce this book, a full bibliography can be found at nationalparkshistory.com.

A project like this is impossible without the support, encouragement, and sacrifices of so many people. First and foremost is my wife, Mikayla. She has supported and encouraged this project from the start, allowing me to spend many evening and weekend hours "locked in my office" researching, writing, and revising. I could not have completed this book without her.

In addition, this book was fueled by the support of all my family members. Katrina always offered words of advise and motivation. Hannah always asks for progress updates while cutting my hair. Kipp read, edited, and re-read many portions of this book. Jay lent his expertise to refining several sections. Additional thanks goes to Chris, Glenn, Kristin, Emma, Cole, and Colin for their encouragement and interest in this project.

I also had support from many people outside my family, particularly in the technical elements of this book. Ann edited this book and offered professional advise. Aubrey designed the cover. John proofread an early version.

A special thanks also goes to the students and teachers I work amongst, whose interest in this work has always motivated me to push on with it.

155

W ILL DE MAN IS a history teacher, writer, and public land advocate in West Michigan. In addition to his two books on the history of the national parks, Will posts regularly on Substack and Instagram, connecting the history of our public lands to the current moment. You can find more from Will on his website, nationalparkshistory.com.